"A heartening and fundamental guide for anyone battling the relentless pressures of modern beauty and health ideals. *Beautiful Freedom* is bursting with Bible-centered wisdom and highlights Christ's love for us. More than insightful information, this book is a soothing balm, offering real hope and freedom that is only found in Jesus Christ. I pray that God will use this book to remind the church that true beauty and freedom are ultimately found in him and not the fleeting standards of the world."

PORTIA COLLINS, Host, *Grounded* Podcast

"Christian women are not exempt from cultural pressures around aging, appearance, and beauty. Stacy Reaoch offers biblical wisdom, truth, and encouragement that soothes the soul of any woman who is stressed out over how she looks, how she should exercise, or what she should eat. This book offers sweet relief and poignant reminders that the most beautiful things about us are not external but eternal."

**HEATHER CREEKMORE,
Host, *Compared to Who?* Podcast**

"Young or old, thick or thin, mostly satisfied or perpetually frustrated by what you see when you look in the mirror: whoever you are, you need an embodied theology, a grid for thinking about your body and beauty that is more than skin-deep. In her thought-provoking book, *Beautiful Freedom*, Stacy Reaoch will help you see yourself through the lens of God's unchanging word. In seeing his heart rightly, you'll finally be able to see yourself and your body choices with hope and freedom. You'll want to share this book with every woman you know."

ERIN DAVIS, Author, *Fasting and Feasting*

HOW THE BIBLE
SHAPES YOUR
VIEW OF APPEARANCE,
FOOD, AND FITNESS

Beautiful Freedom

STACY REAOCH

thegoodbook
COMPANY

To my daughters, Milaina and Annalyse.

May you walk in freedom all your days, enjoying the good gifts God has given and trusting that you are most beautiful when you're most like Christ.

"For freedom Christ has set us free; stand firm therefore, and do not submit again to a yoke of slavery." —Galatians 5:1

Beautiful Freedom
© Stacy Reaoch, 2024

Published by:
The Good Book Company

thegoodbook.com | thegoodbook.co.uk
thegoodbook.com.au | thegoodbook.co.nz | thegoodbook.co.in

Published in association with The Gates Group.

Cover design by Jennifer Phelps | Art direction and design by André Parker

ISBN: 9781784989736 | JOB-007646 | Printed in India

Contents

Introduction

"Lose the weight for good by following these simple food hacks!"

"Look 10 years younger with this amazing new serum!"

"Avoid these 7 foods and add years to your life!"

"Be strong and sexy in just 15 minutes of exercise per day!"

It's no secret that society is obsessed with our outward appearance. People spend thousands of dollars on beauty treatments with the hope of looking a few years younger. Whether it's Botox injections, kale shakes, or a slew of cosmetics, the desire and hope remain the same. The lies of our society tell us that if we can just lose a few pounds, smooth out our wrinkles, or achieve a toned and healthy body, then we'll be happy.

It's hard not to be swept up in the idea that a more attractive and fit physical body will solve our problems in life—whether they have to do with romantic relationships, self-confidence, or sickness. The overwhelming amount of advice about our bodies can leave us worrying about the choices we make—

whether the food we bought is nutritious enough, whether our aging joints will still be able to do all that we want them to. Or, on the other side of the coin, whether the weight we gained from indulging in our favorite foods will keep us from achieving the things we're longing for.

What promises freedom and happiness leaves us trapped in a downward spiral of discontentment. And ultimately, if we're honest, we know that physical beauty will fade and leave us disappointed. We're racing the clock and will inevitably lose.

Yet God is clear that his intention is not for us to worry about our bodies but to trust him (Matthew 6:25-34). The one who cares for the birds in the sky and the flowers in the field cares even more for us. Jesus came to set us free from the power of sin and death. He came to free us from enslavement to all our fears and failures, whatever they are. Jesus gives us hope that we can walk in the freedom, peace, and joy that only he can provide—if we are willing to let him teach us.

"YOU'RE NOT BAD LOOKING"

My own struggle with body image began in the tumultuous teenage years. Even though I had a voracious appetite, the calories couldn't keep up with my growing body. Every time I put on my pom-pom cheerleading uniform, I was embarrassed by my chicken skinny legs. I was always secretly hoping the weather would be cool enough to warrant wearing sweatpants under my skirt or a turtleneck under the sleeveless top. Anything to hide myself a little more.

One particular day stands out to me. As I walked to my desk in school, the eyes of the boy who sat next to me scanned me over from head to toe. "You know, you're not bad looking if you weren't so damn skinny," he said in a matter-of-fact tone.

It's funny how some 30 years later I still remember that remark. I remember how my face flushed with embarrassment as I sank into my seat. I remember wishing my body was more filled out. Thinking that for sure I would land a boyfriend and a date to Homecoming if I just had a few more curves.

As I moved into adulthood and began having children, my struggle swung in the other direction. Even though I never considered myself a "dieter," I occasionally jumped on board with new food rules that were supposed to help keep the weight off. Yet none of these new eating methods actually stuck—likely because they took all the fun out of food and weren't realistic ways to eat with a family.

I've definitely swung on the pendulum—from zealously reading food labels to binging on my kids' Halloween candy. Perhaps this is why as a mom in my mid-forties, when it seems like everything that touches my lips adds to the width of my hips, the body-image battle can still rear its ugly head. Aging is not an easy thing in a culture obsessed with youthful beauty.

But I've also grown in my struggle. I'm learning what it means to age with grace, to find my identity in who Christ says I am versus the reflection in the mirror. To remember that what matters most isn't whether I've gained or lost five pounds, but that I'm living my life for the glory of God.

More than my own story, though, what really led me to write this book was the experience of walking with a number of friends and family members as they battled their own body-image issues—from the everyday grind of living in a culture of comparison, to food addictions and fitness obsessions, to full-blown eating disorders. Some of these women were kind enough to let me interview them as I wrote the book, sharing their stories in hopes of shedding light on the issues at hand and helping others to find the freedom they need.

A RESHAPED PERSPECTIVE

Maybe you can identify with some of the struggles I just outlined. You've jumped from the Keto diet to a vegan diet to throwing out every ounce of sugar in your kitchen. You've lost a few pounds and gained them back, only to find yourself at the start of the vicious cycle again. You've joined the gym, invested way too much in home exercise equipment, and logged every step you take. You eagerly try the latest skincare products in hopes of turning back the hands of time. But still the body you crave seems like an impossible dream. The picture-perfect woman on your exercise app is unattainable.

As Christians, how are we to view all of this? Is the pursuit of physical beauty a legitimate concern? Does God care how I eat? Or if I exercise? How much is too much in terms of the amount of money and time we spend on our bodies? Maybe it's a surprise to you to even start thinking about these things in light of our relationship with God. Yet the truth is that we *can* actively honor him with our bodies.

The Bible doesn't give us black-and-white answers to what we should eat or how much exercise we should do. There are no tips for a great skincare regime in its pages! So you won't find diet formulas or exercise plans in this book. But the kindness of God doesn't leave us without help. The

Bible does give us wisdom and guidance in all of these areas. And with the help of the Holy Spirit, we can trust God to lead us to embrace an eternal perspective that can bring us freedom from our worries and uncertainties.

Our bodies matter to God. He made us intentionally in his image and he knows every hair on our heads (Luke 12:7). He came to dwell among us in his own earthly body in the person of Jesus—redeeming us, body and soul. He lives within our bodies now by his Spirit, if we are trusting in Christ. And one day these broken vessels will be fully restored, without pain or limitations as we worship our God in heaven.

As we explore those amazing truths and more, we start to find ourselves with a new perspective on our bodies and how we treat them. We'll be equipped to really examine our motivations— why do we eat the way we do? Why do we exercise, or not exercise? Why are we inclined to go to great lengths to look a few years younger? Why do we have this tendency or that tendency? And crucially, where is God calling us into something better? In what ways is he inviting us into freedom?

My prayer for you, as you read this book, is that God will grant you new eyes to see your body the way he sees it—as a gift to enjoy and to steward for his glory. I hope that you will start to find freedom from the fears and concerns that weigh you down, and confidence in his sovereign work that knitted you together. And I pray that you will be inspired to love God more. Our Creator is the true source of beauty— fixing our hope on him will never disappoint!

1. A Beautiful Life

What do you think of when you hear the word "beauty"? Do you automatically think of that famous actress with the seemingly never-aging body and flawless skin? The woman on your exercise app who exhibits Hulk-like strength and fortitude? Maybe it's the makeup stashed in your bathroom drawer that promises to erase wrinkles and create a beautiful face. Or maybe you're thinking of some majestic mountains you hiked through on vacation.

I guess all of us want to live what we might call "a beautiful life." You know, the kind of life you see on social media or in magazines. We want to look good and feel good—in our bodies, in our minds, in what we eat and how we dress. But to find *true* beauty, we need to look first at God.

Right now, the change of seasons surrounds me. We are officially in fall, but the temperature still feels like summer. The trees are draped in colorful leaves, billowy clouds float in the blue sky, and the squirrels are chasing each other in my backyard. All of these magnificent scenes are created by our good and sovereign God. He is the one who paints the moon in the sky each night and causes the bright morning sun to rise. He puts the stars in the heavens and knows every hair on every person's head. And he is himself beautiful.

In the book of Psalms, we see David reminding himself of the beauty of God in an unlikely situation: when he is being attacked and pursued by King Saul.

> *"One thing have I asked of the LORD, that will I seek after: that I may dwell in the house of the LORD all the days of my life, to gaze upon the beauty of the LORD and to inquire in his temple." (Psalm 27:4)*

Even in the midst of danger, David doesn't say, *One thing I ask: that I may be safe!* None of the worries of David's life seem to matter in comparison with having a relationship with God. And none of the good things in his life do either. Being made king is nothing compared to the steadfast companionship of the Lord. Impressing others with worldly success doesn't light a candle to being consumed with an infinitely perfect God—because it's not about David, it's about God.

Is that how you and I feel? Not always! And particularly when it comes to issues around our bodies. It's completely natural to want to look good and feel good, but very often that leads us into worry and fear. We worry about our attractiveness, we worry about weight, we worry that our bodies can't do what they used to be able to do, we worry about how healthy we are or aren't. It's easy to become consumed with issues related to our bodies.

Imagine being like David—so taken with God that you can't take your eyes off him, and all those other struggles seem like nothing! Let me ask you: do you think it's possible? Can you be free from body-image issues or counting calories or fearing that you won't be able to fit into the dress in time for the wedding? Can you be free from the fear of aging, of adding a few pounds around your middle, or of going without your favorite food or drink?

The aim of this book is to lead you down a path of freedom. We can learn to put off those things that enslave us and put on the Lord Jesus—so that we too start to merely glance at our worries but gaze and gaze at the Lord. Not only can we grow in a sense of bodily freedom but, in the process, we can learn to love God more.

Are you ready for that?

AN EARLY BATTLE

For some of us, a fixation with our bodies starts early in life. My friend Jill shared her story with me. "My first memory of being concerned about my body image was from when I was just five or six years old. My dad looked at my chubby limbs and said, 'You know, if you want to lose weight, you're really going to have to work at it. Our genes are working against us.'"

Starting in elementary school, Jill began doing workouts and comparing herself to other girls. By eighth grade she was reading food labels and counting calories, scrupulously watching her diet, and enjoying the attention she was getting for her looks. It seemed that the harder she worked at it, the more praise she got. The attention and compliments fueled her desire to lose weight. Jill's battle with perfectionism led her to plastic surgery in her early twenties and a full-blown eating disorder a few years later.

Although she'd been raised in a Christian family, the all-consuming battle for beauty kept Jill's eyes focused on self rather than on God. "Beauty is power," she told me. "It was exhilarating to know I was turning heads each time I walked into the gym." Dating a well-known bodybuilder and entering the world of competitions only added fuel to the fire.

As the praise of others fed her motivation, Jill kept moving down more and more dangerous paths to achieve her goals. A friend who worked in a pharmacy began illegally selling her Adderall, an addictive stimulant that kept her moving at a fast pace, feeling little need for sleep or food. But soon Jill's body began to crash and she realized just how far she'd fallen—all in the name of health and fitness.

I also think about my friend Amy, who grew up with a mom obsessed with dieting. Amy's mom never walked by a mirror without stopping to notice her reflection and make a self-deprecating comment: "I look so old!" or "I look bigger each time I look in the mirror!" Watching her mom jump from diet to diet and be consumed with her body image contributed to Amy having a distorted view of her own body. It seemed like the goal of life was to be thin, young, and beautiful. Wasn't that why her mom was always talking about diets, calories, and weight?

There are so many causes of our struggles with body image. Maybe we're like Jill: someone close to us once said a hurtful comment about the way we look. Maybe we fear not being loved for who we are. Maybe we worry about not being healthy or strong enough. Or we've spent too much time online, looking at filtered images of fitness gurus that make us feel like we're not up to snuff. Our struggles might be embedded in low self-esteem or compounded by mental illness.

For Jill, these struggles took a relatively extreme form; for many of us it's much more subtle. Maybe you never feel like your body is good enough. Or your time at the gym is spent comparing your body to the woman's next to yours who seems perfectly fit. Or you feel out of control with the food around you. You may not be ready to get plastic surgery or forgo your favorite foods, but there is a constant grating in your mind over what's wrong with your body.

Our culture is quick to point out solutions to our problems. The beauty industry bombards us with advertisements for the latest and greatest serums or injections which promise to turn back time. The fitness industry offers every workout we can imagine—from hot yoga to Zumba to HIIT, available at any time or place that fits your schedule. Diet and wellness culture assures us that we'll lose our extra pounds and add years to our lives as long as we adhere to their rules and cut out carbs, sugar, or processed foods. All of these quick-fix solutions offer supposedly easy answers to our worries about our bodies.

But as Christians, our approach to fitness, health, and beauty needs to be different. I don't mean that hot yoga is out the window or that you should stop paying attention to your appearance: what I mean is that we need to take stock of our baseline assumptions about our bodies. We need to start by thinking about what the Bible says—and when we do, we'll find that God has different ideas about what really, truly constitutes "a beautiful life."

TRUE BEAUTY

Beauty is defined as "the quality present in a thing or person that gives intense pleasure or deep satisfaction to the mind, whether arising from sensory manifestations (as shape, color, sound, etc.), a meaningful design or pattern, or something else (as a personality in which high spiritual qualities are manifest)."[1] *Intense pleasure or deep satisfaction to the mind.* Maybe you've enjoyed the beauty of a pink sunset. Or you've marveled at the intricacies of a hand-sewn quilt. It's undeniable: God created us as people who delight in beauty.

God, as our Creator, is the source of all physical beauty—but he himself is also the most magnificent display of beauty. This might sound strange—didn't Jesus die a gruesome and horrific death on the cross? In what sense is he a marvelous display of beauty? Remember that beauty is more than outward appearance. Our definition of beauty says that it can arise from something like a person's character or personality.

That's what we think about when it comes to God's beauty: his character. We can meditate on his boundless mercy that gave us new life in Christ—and not by any of our own doing, but by his grace alone. No amount of good deeds or kind thoughts can give us redemption from our sin, but only Jesus! What a marvelous, undeserved gift. We were once dead but are now alive! Isn't that beautiful?

> *"But God, being rich in mercy, because of the great love with which he loved us, even when we were dead in our trespasses, made us alive together with Christ—by grace you have been saved."*
>
> *(Ephesians 2:4-5)*

I remember reading the Bible for the very first time as a new believer in college. One day as I was sitting in my dorm room soaking up the parable of the lost sheep in Luke 15:1-7, I was overcome with God's love for me. Tears spilled over as I realized that *I* was the lost sheep that had been found. Jesus' love became so real to me—a beautiful display of the life-changing power of the gospel. God was giving me joy in things that I'd never experienced before! My eyes were open to new spiritual realities, and my newfound faith in Christ propelled me to share the good news with all the college students I knew (no matter how crazy I might have seemed).

Jesus Christ came to earth as a baby, suffered, bled, and died to take away our sin. His perfect obedience to the Father and his excruciating death on the cross paved the way for his enemies to be made friends. When we ponder what Jesus has done for us, freeing us from this dark world and giving us eternal life in him, we realize that he is the essence of beauty. His love is made manifest by his death and resurrection:

> *"God shows his love for us in that while we were still sinners, Christ died for us." (Romans 5:8)*

And this beauty doesn't just inspire us: it changes us. When we are in Christ, our Father sees us as he sees Jesus. We are holy in God's sight, blameless and unblemished (Colossians 1:22). This matters hugely! Maybe you feel ugly or fear being unloved. Or maybe you are in pain or frustrated by your body. Remind yourself that you already give pleasure and satisfaction to our heavenly Father. You *are* loved. You *are* beautiful.

REFLECTIONS OF BEAUTY

This beauty that Jesus has given us isn't just about how God sees us, crucial though that is. It also makes a difference to how we interact with others. As Christians, made new by the Holy Spirit, we can start to reflect God's beauty in new ways to those around us. The truth is that we are most beautiful when we are most like God—when we reflect the character of God.

Let's think about the story of Naomi and her daughter-in-law Ruth in the Old Testament. Ruth and Naomi had come upon a challenging time of life: they were both left destitute by the deaths of the male members of their family. Despite Naomi's pleas for Ruth to go back to live with her parents, where she had a better chance of finding prosperity again, Ruth insisted on staying beside her mother-in-law:

> *"Do not urge me to leave you or to return from following you. For where you go I will go, and where you lodge I will lodge. Your people shall be my people, and your God my God. Where you die I will die, and there will I be buried." (Ruth 1:16-17)*

Ruth follows her mother-in-law, even though it doesn't seem like a very wise or hopeful thing to do. Why? Because of her steadfast faith in God. Ruth is gazing at God and putting him before her own personal concerns.

As the story goes on, a ray of hope in the two women's lives is the possibility of finding a husband for Ruth—since in those days women had very little security without a man to protect them. Enter Boaz. Despite Ruth being from the land of Moab (Moabites would have been considered an enemy of God's people), Boaz shows extraordinary kindness by allowing Ruth to glean in his fields, even telling her to stay close to his workers, who can provide protection for her (Ruth 2:8-9).

You might wonder what attracted Boaz to Ruth. Why would he show this stranger such kindness? Did Ruth have a beautiful face or a supermodel's body? Although we're unsure of what Ruth looked like, we are confident of one thing: Boaz was drawn to Ruth because of the kindness of her heart. Look at this interaction between them in Ruth 2:10-12:

> *"Then she fell on her face, bowing to the ground, and said to him, 'Why have I found favor in your eyes, that you should take notice of me, since I am a foreigner?' But Boaz answered her, 'All that you have done for your mother-in-law since the death of your husband has been fully told to me, and how you left your father and mother and your native land and came to a people that you did not know before. The* LORD *repay you for what you have done, and a full reward be given you by the* LORD*, the God of Israel, under whose wings you have come to take refuge!'"*

What does Boaz admire? He notices the sacrificial love that Ruth shows to her mother-in-law, her willingness to give up a more comfortable life in her own land with her own family. The compassion of God shines through Ruth's words and actions. Her faith in God and the fruit of kindness in her life are a reflection of God's own character.

As the story goes on, Naomi recognizes the opportunity that Ruth has here. She gives what might seem like shady advice, telling Ruth to wash, put on perfume and a cloak and go down to the threshing floor at night to lay beside Boaz. It's a delicate way for Ruth to ask Boaz to marry her.

It's interesting to note that Ruth's appearance isn't completely irrelevant. She is concerned to dress well and be physically attractive when the moment comes. Sometimes we think that to be truly spiritual we have to not care about those things, but this isn't true! Even so, although Naomi's advice focused on the external—Ruth's appearance and attractive scent—Boaz's glad acceptance was focused on the character of her heart.

> *"May you be blessed by the LORD, my daughter. You*
> *have made this last kindness greater than the first*
> *in that you have not gone after young men, whether*
> *poor or rich. And now, my daughter, do not fear.*
> *I will do for you all that you ask, for all my fellow*
> *townsmen know that you are a worthy woman."*
> *(Ruth 3:10-11)*

The world tells us that our physical appearance—our skin, our strength, our youthfulness—is what makes us beautiful. But the story of Boaz and Ruth reminds us that true beauty is displayed through our hearts. Boaz was drawn to the kindness and compassion Ruth displayed to her mother-in-law. In effect, Ruth was reflecting God's own kindness—and this made her truly beautiful.

FINDING FREEDOM

We hear this point echoed in Peter's first letter, where he addresses wives married to unbelieving husbands:

"Do not let your adorning be external—the braiding of hair and the putting on of gold jewelry, or the clothing you wear—but let your adorning be the hidden person of the heart with the imperishable beauty of a gentle and quiet spirit, which in God's sight is very precious." (1 Peter 3:3-4)

Peter recognizes the temptation women face to be consumed with their outward appearance. He wants us to focus our efforts not on our physical selves so much as on growing in godliness. This will impact our relationships far more significantly than the latest styles of dress or hair—and may even win unbelieving husbands to Christ. A heart focused on God has a quiet confidence that extends beyond the reflection in the mirror. It's true, sadly, that growing in inner beauty may not be valued by all people; but it is valued by God. And it's his opinion that matters more than anyone else's.

Remember my friend Jill? By God's grace she came to know our Savior and realized that her identity isn't found in having the best body at the gym. She didn't need the approval of her father, or of others, but only needed the approval of God. Even though body image will likely always be something of a struggle for her, Jill has been set free from a deep enslavement to exercise and weight loss. She knows that her firm foundation is found in the truth of the gospel. Jesus sees Jill as beautiful, and as she gazes at him day by day, he is transforming her to be more like himself. She is finding freedom as her trust in God grows. She is beholding his beauty instead of striving for physical perfection.

The message here isn't that physical stuff doesn't matter at all. Christians are free to enjoy makeup, clothing, fitness workouts, clean-eating plans—and French fries. But *free* is an important word in that sentence! So often we don't feel free but trapped by our concerns about our bodies. Gazing at the beauty of Jesus doesn't mean we will never think about our appearance again, but it does mean we will stop being enslaved by it.

GRATEFUL FOR A GOOD BODY

We've talked about beauty being more than just our physical appearance, but a big question remains: how then do we think about our physical selves? God gave each of us a physical body to live our lives on earth. And the body is significant.

We're going to delve more into what the Bible says about our bodies in later chapters. But for now, let's note that God created man and woman in his own image (Genesis 1:27). He knit each of us together in our mother's womb, knowing every hair on our heads. David proclaims in Psalm 139:13-14 that we are "fearfully and wonderfully made." That means no matter what size or shape you've been given, your body was intentionally designed by God. It may or may not fit into our culture's view of what is beautiful, but God says that it is very good (Genesis 1:31)!

The Bible never commands us to be thin. Or to have toned arms. Or to have a great workout routine. These are cultural ideals that we often place on ourselves. We focus on so-called flaws—wishing that our nose was smaller or that our hair was thicker or our legs slenderer. But God wants us to be thankful for the body he has given us. The God of the universe proclaimed it "good" just as he made it.

So: what if instead of complaining and worrying about

our physical appearance, we made an intentional effort to be grateful to God for our bodies? What if we chose to let our bodies draw us to worship?

Consider the spectrum of things your body can do—from walking and running to talking and reading, tasting and seeing. Maybe you are all too aware of the limitations of your body—it can't do all the things you want it to. But it still can do *something*, and it was carefully designed by God. Instead of lamenting that you can hardly walk a mile without huffing and puffing, could you thank God that you have the ability and strength to walk that mile? Instead of complaining about your tall stature, could you thank God for the unique perks that come with it—like being able to reach for things on the highest shelf, or help someone stuff their luggage in an overhead bin on the plane? (On behalf of all the short people in the world, thank you…) Or, to get more serious: even if you're living with a physical disability, can you thank God for the way your blood pumps around your veins without you having to tell it to, or the way your lungs keep you breathing, or the way your skin can feel the touch of someone who loves you?

When our bodies rise out of bed each morning and go to bed each night, we can offer our thanks to God for all that he allowed us to accomplish throughout the day. A thankful heart is good medicine. And focusing on the gift of our bodies changes our perspective from one of complaining and discontentment to one of praise. We're starting to gaze at God, not at ourselves—and once again, that's true beauty.

THE ULTIMATE SOURCE OF BEAUTY

There is freedom when we gaze at God and see his beauty, because we realize that his beauty is also our beauty. It's not that our health, fitness, and diet don't matter. But they don't matter most. The life-changing power of Jesus in our lives promises freedom. We can bank on the truth that God loves us and intricately knit our bodies together in a way that brings glory and honor to him.

> *"Now the Lord is the Spirit, and where the Spirit of the Lord is, there is freedom. And we all, with unveiled face, beholding the glory of the Lord, are being transformed into the same image from one degree of glory to another." (2 Corinthians 3:17-18)*

Freedom from body-image struggles is possible! And focusing our lives on knowing and loving the God of the universe is the way we can start to find it.

FOR REFLECTION OR DISCUSSION

1. What do you think of when you hear the word "beauty"?

2. How would you describe your attitude toward your physical self? How have your life experiences shaped the way you think about your body or the way you treat it?

3. In what sense is God the most magnificent display of beauty? How could this impact our understanding of what beauty is?

4. God tells us in Genesis 1:31 that everything he made was very good, including our bodies! What makes you personally grateful for the body God has given you? How do you think you might grow in gratitude?

2. Whose Kingdom Are You Seeking?

Morgan loved all things beauty-related from the time she was a little girl. From the latest Barbie dolls to pretend makeup to noticing the newest fashions on TV, Morgan was hooked. Before she was even allowed to wear makeup, she found chapsticks with a hint of color, put Vaseline on her eyelids to make them shine, and pinched her cheeks in hopes of adding a rosy glow to her face. It was fun!

As Morgan entered the teen years, her desire for beauty grew. She was constantly comparing herself to other girls on social media. Hair highlights, workouts designed to create a buff body, and tanning booths became a staple part of her diet. As Morgan entered adulthood and realized that she would not always have the body of a 16-year-old, the pressure to be thin became more overwhelming. Soon the money and time Morgan invested in her pursuit of beauty became a drain on her family, with both her husband and kids resenting how consumed she was with her appearance. It was a never-ending pit of chasing beauty and youth.

Heidi is a self-proclaimed wellness guru. She religiously does her 6am workout each morning and finishes it with a kale protein shake. Heidi is always on the lookout for the latest supplements and vitamins that promise stronger muscles, thicker hair, and great health. And she loves to experiment with recipes that give her the most energy for her busy days. Wherever Heidi is—at school picking up her kids, in the church fellowship hall, or chatting over the fence with her neighbor—you can bet you'll hear conversations about her latest exercise routine or the most nutritious foods you can eat.

But sometimes Heidi's friends wish they could have a conversation that doesn't revolve around the best new blenders for shakes or the superfoods that can fix all their problems. Heidi's passion for wellness seems to supersede everything else in life. It started off as something positive, but perhaps it isn't anymore.

In the last chapter we focused on freedom. We thought about how God is the source of beauty, how he made our bodies good, and how we become truly beautiful when we focus our lives on him. In Chapter 3 we'll talk more about what that looks like—reminding ourselves that God cares about our bodies and thinking about how we can honor him with them. But first we need to take an honest look at how our concern about our bodies can start to lead us astray.

I wonder whether you feel you have anything in common with Morgan or Heidi. Maybe you do: you recognize that your attitude toward beauty or your body has got out of control, and you want help. Or maybe not—you're not *always* talking about this stuff, after all. You're not *that* obsessive. You just have a few worries from time to time.

Wherever you're at, it's worth taking time to examine and challenge yourself about your actions and attitudes—because in order to find freedom from our struggles, we need to get real about them. We need to think carefully about the unhelpful patterns of thought we've gotten into, and how our focus on body issues may have drawn us away from gazing at God. We need to realize where we've fallen into sin and where we need to repent and ask for help to change.

This chapter will challenge you! But it will also be a vital step on your path toward freedom.

THE GREATEST COMMANDMENT

What worries you about your body? All of us likely have concerns that run through our minds. *What if I'm too busy to fit in my workout today? What if my chest is too flat or my lips are too thin? What if I can't lose weight? What if I'm not pretty enough and I never get married, or my husband is no longer attracted to me? What if I can't fit into the dress I'm dying to wear? What if the food I ate at the church potluck harms my body?*

Jesus knew we would be tempted to be fearful and anxious over our bodies and our physical needs. And he took the time to talk about these issues in a way that should both comfort and challenge us.

> *"Therefore I tell you, do not be anxious about your life, what you will eat or what you will drink, nor about your body, what you will put on. Is not life more than food, and the body more than clothing? Look at the birds of the air: they neither sow nor reap nor gather into barns, and yet your heavenly*

> *Father feeds them. Are you not of more value than*
> *they? And which of you by being anxious can add a*
> *single hour to his span of life?" (Matthew 6:25-27)*

Jesus gives us the example of God providing food for something as small as birds. They are so fragile, and yet God feeds them. How much more will he provide for us, who are so much more valuable in his eyes than a tiny bird? Jesus is saying that God has your back! He might not provide exactly what you want, but he will provide exactly what you need.

Then Jesus talks about flowers:

> *"And why are you anxious about clothing? Consider*
> *the lilies of the field, how they grow: they neither*
> *toil nor spin, yet I tell you, even Solomon in all his*
> *glory was not arrayed like one of these. But if God so*
> *clothes the grass of the field, which today is alive and*
> *tomorrow is thrown into the oven, will he not much*
> *more clothe you, O you of little faith?" (v 28-30)*

I'm struck that Jesus doesn't just talk about basic necessities here. He doesn't just say that God allows the flowers to grow. He says that they are splendid and glorious—more impressively clothed than Solomon, the richest king in Israel's history. If you think that God doesn't care about beauty, think again: he is the one who clothes the fields with flowers!

Jesus is also reminding us a second time that we don't need to be concerned about our physical selves. Whether it's basic necessities like food or water or more complex anxieties around how people perceive us or how healthy we feel, we can be confident that God knows our needs. We don't have to worry.

To help us, Jesus lifts our eyes upward and gives us a new priority instead:

> *"But seek first the kingdom of God and his righteousness, and all these things will be added to you." (v 33)*

Seeking God and living our lives to bring glory to him is the highest purpose of life. This command is also echoed in Matthew 6:10, when Jesus teaches us to say, "Your kingdom come, your will be done, on earth as it is in heaven." Seeking the Lord's will above our own helps us keep an eternal perspective. We won't get caught up in the next big fad or be consumed with dropping ten pounds, because our hearts and minds are fixed on bigger things. And when we get our priorities straight, we start to realize that God is showering us with blessing every day.

Jesus' words are an invitation to trust our God—but they are also a challenge to our old way of thinking. It's hard for us to admit, but we need to see that when we get consumed in our own worries, we are not seeking God's kingdom first. We're seeking our own kingdom instead—and that is a form of idolatry.

LOVE GONE WRONG

The word "idol" might conjure up pictures of golden calves or statues of foreign gods. Yet idolatry begins long before we craft an image of gold to bow down to. Idolatry often begins with good desires—maybe a desire for marriage or children, for career success, ministry opportunities, or a healthy body. But those good desires can become too important in our lives, something we feel like we can't live without. Elyse Fitzpatrick defines idolatry as "love gone wrong":

"Idols are the thoughts, desires, longings, and expectations that we worship in the place of the true God. Idols cause us to ignore the true God in search of what we think we need."[2]

Idolatry is taking a good desire and making it ultimate. It's believing that you can only be happy or content when you get what you want, not what God provides. Can you see how this is the opposite of what Jesus was encouraging us to do in Matthew 6?

We all struggle with forms of idolatry. For some of us it's money; for others, it's obedient children, or the perfect marriage, or physical beauty. Idolatry is a slippery slope because it takes something that is often good and twists it into something harmful. Pastor and author Tim Keller warns us of this paradox:

"We think that idols are bad things, but that is almost never the case. The greater the good, the more likely we are to expect that it can satisfy our deepest needs and hopes. Anything can serve as a counterfeit god, especially the very best things in life."[3]

Think about idolatry as it relates to beauty. With each passing day, our bodies are changing—and not always in the way we want. I routinely see a new gray hair that's popped up or a line on my face that I didn't notice before. Is it sinful to use age-repairing night cream or makeup to enhance the appearance of my face? I don't think so. Unless it becomes an all-consuming desire; one that inordinately consumes my thoughts, time and resources.

To be perfectly honest, this is something that I battle. It's easy to go to the pool or beach and notice the thin and toned bodies all around me—to wonder how that mom doesn't seem to have an ounce of fat on her or wonder what her workout routine is. But when I start comparing myself to others, I can easily slide down the slippery slope of discontentment, thinking my own body isn't good enough, or thin enough, or strong enough. When our thoughts become consumed with our appearance, new diet, or exercise regimen, we've fallen into the trap of idolatry. We're focusing on our own little kingdom and not on our God's.

RACHEL'S DISAPPOINTMENTS

Consider the story of Rachel in Genesis 29 – 31. She was the chosen wife, the one known for her beauty, the favorite of her husband (Genesis 29:17-18). But despite all her blessings, she carried the weight of an unfulfilled longing: the desire for children. What made it even harder was that Rachel's sister, Leah (who was also married to the same husband, Jacob— yikes!), was blessed with seven children, while Rachel had none. Can you imagine what Rachel must have felt as she watched her sister get pregnant again and again? Anyone who has struggled to conceive knows the crushing disappointment each month when you realize that you still aren't pregnant. And Leah didn't make things any easier. She competed with Rachel over their husband's attention (Genesis 30:15-16), rubbing it in that she had a growing number of offspring while Rachel remained childless.

Rachel had a good and godly desire to be a mother. She desired to nurture, love, and raise her own child—to impart her faith and family traditions to the next generation. To embrace the calling given by God to so many women. Yet that desire became all-consuming. Instead of trusting that God was in control of her fertility, she absurdly blamed her husband, turning on him with anger and bitterness: "Give me children, or I shall die!" (Genesis 30:1).[4]

Rachel's disappointments led her to despair. And she didn't stop there. Her desire for a child led her to give her servant, Bilhah, as another wife to Jacob, in hopes of gaining a surrogate child through her. It's a demonstration that sin never just affects one person. It's a web that is weaved larger and larger, and it entraps others along the way.

When our eyes become clouded with our fleshly desires, it keeps us from seeing the goodness of God. Even after God remembered Rachel and opened her womb, blessing her with her son, Joseph, she became discontent with only one child—"May the LORD add to me another son!" she prayed (Genesis 30:24). She died while giving birth to her second son, Benjamin, whom she named Ben-Oni, meaning "son of my sorrow" (Genesis 35:18). Even in her last moments on earth, Rachel was lamenting what she didn't have. Her insatiable desire had consumed her life to the bitter end.

This is idolatry, "love gone wrong." Rachel started with the good desire to be a mother, but it got twisted and deformed along the way.

None of us want to be like Rachel—absorbed with our own desires to the point of sinful actions and words. We want to be contented and godly women, not bitter and self-obsessed! But this type of idolatry is a slippery slope. So we need to take a careful look at ourselves, and ask for God's help in revealing where we're going astray. We can trust our faithful heavenly Father to guide our hearts in the process and not withhold anything good from our lives (Psalm 84:11).

SQUEEZING OUT GOD

As I was shopping for a birthday card once, I overheard a conversation between two employees in the store I was in. One woman was sharing some health concerns she had. The other was quick to offer a solution: "I have a quinoa cookie recipe that will *blow your mind!*" I couldn't help but smile at the woman's enthusiasm for her recipe. (For some reason, the words "quinoa" and "cookie" don't seem to go together in the same sentence for me...) But at the same time, I realized she wasn't really listening or offering any sympathy to her friend with health concerns. Instead she just rattled on about how certain foods had impacted her own life and could definitely be the source of her friend's problem.

Sometimes our preoccupation with our bodies and diets can bleed into every conversation we have. We don't even realize how consumed we are with thoughts about food and health. Instead of listening empathetically to our friend's problems, we're thinking of the solution we can offer through our own diet and supplements. Or instead of hanging out and embracing what someone else wants to do, we let ourselves be held back by worries about how we'll look or what we'll eat. And we miss out on truly being a caring and considerate friend.

We long to be caught up in worship at church, but we end up being distracted by looking at other women's clothes or hair. We long to be part of a community, but concerns about what food we can eat hold us back from participating in church events. We long to be more prayerful, but we can't deal with not having a makeup regime or a workout each morning—and that pushes out any time for prayer.

You can see how longing for the perfect body or an obsession with the perfect diet can end up squeezing out God—because we're following our own plan for happiness instead of following him. We can think that in order to find a sense of significance, we need to fit into a smaller dress size. We idolize organic food, thinking that controlling every ounce of food that we consume will ensure us good health or a pain-free life. Or we might use an excess of food to numb the pain or stress we're feeling. Maybe exercise is so important to you that you feel like your day is ruined if you haven't fit in your workout— your happiness depends on it. There are so many ways we take the good gifts of food, exercise, and beauty and warp them into mini-idols of our hearts.

Idolatry begins in our imaginations: we dwell on what we perceive to be the perfect circumstance, pine over what we don't have, and become angry or bitter at the lack in our lives. Instead of recognizing God's all-sufficient grace, wisdom, and sovereignty, we think our plan is better. Like Rachel, we see our situation as a curse instead of noticing the blessings God has poured out on us. And what's the result? We miss out on God-given opportunities to showcase his love, because we're naval-gazing at our own lives. And we miss out on experiencing the joy of delighting in God himself, because we're trying to satisfy ourselves in one hundred other ways.

These issues are complicated, and there are lots of reasons why we end up falling into this trap! Maybe you've battled health issues or you've felt the wound of degrading comments made about your appearance when you were young. Maybe disappointments in other areas of life have led you to obsess over the things you can control. Maybe you worry about how people perceive you or you're desperate to make a romantic relationship work.

Remember, your heavenly Father knows exactly what you need (Matthew 6:32). He cares for you! He loves you just as you are, with all your fears and failures. But he also calls you to fix your eyes on him.

THERE IS FREEDOM

The good news is that if we are in Christ, God is still willing to welcome us home even when we have fallen into idolatry. He doesn't want us to miss out. He always wants to give us more of himself. And as Psalm 103:10-11 so beautifully reminds us, his love covers all our sin:

> *"He does not deal with us according to our sins, nor repay us according to our iniquities. For as high as the heavens are above the earth, so great is his steadfast love toward those who fear him."*

God doesn't give us what we deserve, but instead covers us in the precious blood of Christ, seeing us as righteous even when we're far from it. This is why, when we devote ourselves to building his kingdom, we're freed from the self-conscious thoughts that keep us in bondage. We find our joy in serving others, looking to meet their needs and using our gifts to draw others into a relationship with Christ. We find our joy in God himself, knowing he is our redeemer, savior, and friend. These things are far more satisfying than the fleeting pursuit of chasing beauty or health.

Let me encourage you to really examine your heart. Most of us have hidden idols that we don't recognize. Ask God to reveal what you are loving more than him. Here are a few questions to help you diagnose what might be an idol in your life:

- What do I feel like I can't live without?
- What do I need in order to be happy or complete?
- What makes me angry or bitter?
- What do I feel entitled to, and how do I respond when I don't get it?
- Where does my mind go during "down time"? What do I daydream about?

These are convicting questions, and my own answers show me how far I myself need to go in battling idolatry!

But I'm so thankful that Jesus doesn't leave us to fight this battle on our own. He is our great high priest who sympathizes with our weaknesses and assures of help in our time of need (Hebrews 4:14-16). We're promised that he equips us with everything we need for life and godliness (2 Peter 1:3). So let's hit our knees and wage war against our sin! Seeing our sin for what it is paves the way to confession. When we humble ourselves before others and our almighty God, he brings healing to our lives. James 5:16 says, "Confess your sins to one another and pray for one another, that you may be healed."

But we don't stop there. True confession is accompanied by repentance—turning away from our sin. Explaining this to my kids, I like to use the illustration of stinky trash. When we confess our sin (a pile of trash), we make a 180-degree turn the other way and leave that stinky trash in the dust! So, we plead with God to help us find our satisfaction in him instead of our outward appearance. We ask him to give us self-control with food, and wisdom to know how to navigate tempting situations. We ask him to help us keep a God-centered perspective on exercise, so that we're keeping fit not to show off our six-pack on the beach but to use our strength and agility to serve others for his kingdom.

We're going to talk in much more detail about all of this in later chapters, exploring specific situations and figuring out how we can honor God with our bodies instead of becoming trapped by idolatry or fear. But for now, let's remember one thing about our longings and desires: there is a better answer to them. The best way of removing an idol from our lives for good is to make sure we replace it with Jesus. As Tim Keller wrote:

"Jesus must become more beautiful to your imagination, more attractive to your heart, than your idol. This is what will replace your counterfeit gods."[5]

It's not just about removing the idol from our life but *replacing* it with the only source of true satisfaction: the love of Christ. He must be our supreme joy! We don't want a quick fix—like pulling the yellow flower off the dandelion, but leaving the root in the ground to resurface in a couple days. We want to dig up the idol by its roots, uncover how it got there in the first place, and plant something new there instead. Something much more beautiful and much more satisfying.

GIVING GOD GLORY

I want to close by sharing the story of my friend Sadie, who told me her own story of finding freedom from the trap of body idolatry. Sadie struggled with weight and body image from the time she was in elementary school. "I remember being the slowest runner as we ran laps around the gym. I compared myself to the other girls and felt self-conscious about my weight." Sadie's mom was a chronic dieter, always ready to try the next best way to lose weight—kale shakes, low carb and vegan being just a few methods. "My mom modeled discontentment with the way she looked. Foods were labeled as bad or good, and whether she indulged in them determined the quality of her day."

One summer as a college student, Sadie decided to take charge of her weight through vigorous workouts and calorie restriction. It became her mission to shed the pounds, and she returned to college with a new slender body. "I was given lots of praise and accolades for how thin I was. It put me on a trajectory of dieting and grueling exercise routines in order to keep the weight off." Sadie rode that trajectory throughout her new marriage and the birth of her three daughters. But her determination to lose the weight after the third baby became dangerous. She became so thin, her period stopped for nine months. "My hormones were so messed up—it was affecting my emotions and the way I treated my family. I was a scary person." Both Sadie and her husband knew she needed help. The pursuit of health and thinness was destroying their family.

After multiple medical interventions, mentoring, and lots of growth in Sadie's understanding of God's design for our bodies, she finally started to find a healthier attitude toward her diet. Now Sadie tries to listen to her body for signs of hunger, doesn't restrict her calories, and enjoys all kinds and types of food, modeling to her three daughters a healthy perspective on food and body image. She may not be perfect, but she is learning, and relying on the Lord to guide her in the process. She told me, "My body is a gift from God, and I want to give him glory by how I use it and care for it."

You know, the kingdom of self will inevitably crash and burn. These bodies aren't made to last. I'm reminded of that each time my joints ache after a jog or my back stiffens after sitting too long! We live in a fallen world. We get sick. Our bodies age. We slow down and fail to achieve physical perfection. But the kingdom of God will triumph and be a source of eternal peace and joy.

So: whose kingdom are you seeking? What will you do today to take your eyes off of yourself and lift them to heaven—to the God of the universe, who knows your needs? He is the one who is worthy of our eternal worship. And his kingdom is the one that will truly last.

FOR REFLECTION OR DISCUSSION

1. Do you recognize any unhealthy patterns you're struggling with in relation to your body?

2. Read Matthew 6:25-34. What is Jesus' antidote to worry about our bodies? How do you think you could put this antidote into practice?

3. Elyse Fitzpatrick defines idols as "the thoughts, desires, longings, and expectations that we worship in the place of the true God." How can issues with our bodies become idols in our lives? What idols have you personally identified?

4. How does Jesus help us battle our idolatry? (See Hebrews 4:14-16; 2 Peter 1:3; James 5:16.)

3. Apathy, Obsession, and a Healthy Balance

I can be a real pendulum swinger. Sometimes—usually when life feels overwhelming, I'm lacking good sleep, and feel like there's not enough hours in the day—I become apathetic. My flannel PJs, Netflix, and a bowl of ice-cream sound a whole lot more comforting than a trip to the gym. It can be hard to have the motivation to wear something other than yoga pants and a ponytail. But at other times in life, often when things seem to be going fairly well, I've swung too far in the other direction—being overly rigid in my workouts, the number of calories I'm consuming, or what the scale reads in the morning.

Apathy or obsession. So often it seems to be one or the other, doesn't it? And these swings of the pendulum can have a spiritual dimension too.

My friend Jenny is a wife and mom, serving in full-time ministry with her husband. She desires to seek God's kingdom first—and, as part of that, she seeks to remain physically fit. She sees this as a way to honor the Lord with her body and steward it well. After all, we will have more energy to serve God's people if we remain active! Yet Jenny's desire to be fit has become an all-consuming lifestyle. Her kids bemoan the next diet she takes part in as she clears the house of all the "bad foods" she's not allowed to have. Her workout routine keeps getting longer. And each day she watches the numbers on the scale, her emotions riding on whether she's gained or lost a pound. The original good desire that Jenny had, to be physically fit to serve the Lord, has been twisted into living a life that's consumed with her outward appearance.

Meanwhile, Sarah leads a busy life as a single woman caring for her aging parents. She's a business owner and church deacon. To Sarah, seeking God's kingdom is all about throwing herself into caring for others in various spheres of life. Yet she feels exhausted and depleted as she tries to meet so many demands on her time. Instead of preparing a healthy lunch to take with her to work, it's easier to stop at the local fast-food joint for a quick burger and fries. She thinks about exercising after she gets home from work, but then her elderly parents need her attention. Looking after them keeps her spare time full. Not to mention evening church meetings.

Both women started with a desire to seek God's kingdom, but neither of them are managing to find balance when it comes to their bodies. For Jenny, looking after her physical self has become an end in itself, rather than a means to an end: she's lost sight of her original intention to put God and his people first. Meanwhile, Sarah is so focused on her purpose of serving others that she is ignoring the limits of the physical body God gave her. And neither of them is very happy.

Can you identify? In our fast-paced world with an over-emphasis on the externals, it can be easy to get caught up in either situation. We're constantly pushed to do more, be more productive, and keep an attractive figure while doing it all. As Christians, we're exhorted in Scripture to put others' needs ahead of our own (Philippians 2:3-4)—but sometimes we end up pushing ourselves to the point of exhaustion.

So, how do we find a healthy balance? What *did* God intend for our bodies? This chapter aims to answer those questions.

BODY AND SOUL

We spoke in chapter 1 about how our bodies were made good by God. He made us deliberately in his image! But in the New Testament, we get an update. If we trust in Christ, our bodies aren't just good, they're temples of the Holy Spirit.

> *"Or do you not know that your body is a temple of the Holy Spirit within you, whom you have from God? You are not your own, for you were bought with a price. So glorify God in your body."*
> *(1 Corinthians 6:19-20)*

What does it really mean that our bodies are temples of the Holy Spirit? Think back to the Old Testament book of Exodus. The Israelites were given a command to build the tabernacle, where the presence of God would dwell (Exodus 25:8). It was the meeting place with God, where sacrifices would be offered for sin and forgiveness granted.

The tabernacle, which later became a temple during the reign of Solomon (1 Kings 3:8), was a holy place to worship and meet with God. God gave extremely detailed instructions about how to build and care for the tabernacle—with ornate designs featuring precious metals and expensive fabrics. Specific groups of people were given charge over various areas. The Levites were responsible for carrying and setting up the tabernacle as the Israelites made their 40-year trek through the wilderness (Numbers 3 – 4). It was an incredibly important job!

Yet when Jesus came to earth, he removed the need for the temple to be the only meeting place with God. Because of his death and resurrection, believers in Christ were given the third Person of the Godhead, the Holy Spirit, to dwell in our bodies.

What an amazing privilege to have the Spirit of God living inside of us! Think about it this way: you are hosting a person whom you deeply love, respect, and care about. It makes me remember when my husband and I were dating long-distance in college. When Ben rented a car and drove over five hours to see me, I wanted everything to be perfect. I spent time cooking a delicious meal (with very limited culinary skills!), I cleaned my apartment, I got out my best dishes, and I made things as welcoming as possible. I gave thought and effort to what I was wearing and how I fixed my hair and makeup. In a similar way, when we think about hosting the Spirit of God within us, we want to make a special effort to make the most of our bodies, to use them well—because even from a physical standpoint, we are representing the Spirit of God.

1 Corinthians 6:20 urges us, "Glorify God in your body."

Just think: your body, with all its imperfections and flaws, can glorify God! Our bodies—not just our souls—were bought with the precious blood of Jesus! And so as followers of Christ we want to be set apart from the world, using our bodies in ways that bring honor and glory to God. This is our purpose in life.

But it isn't just about what we do with our bodies—it's also about what we do *to* them. Just as the Levites were to carefully and fastidiously care for the beautiful temple, so we are to carefully steward the bodies God has given us. We need to look after them if we are going to use them for his glory.

Both Jenny and Sarah are partially on the right track—but only partially. Jenny's emphasis on caring for her body is an acknowledgment that her physical self matters to God. She wants to be fit and well so that she can use her body to glorify God in lots of different ways. Meanwhile Sarah has understood that part of glorifying God is serving others, just as Christ served us. She pours herself out for others, making genuine sacrifices along the way. It shows that her purpose in life is not about herself but about her Lord and Savior.

Yet neither Jenny nor Sarah seems to have found an attitude to their bodies that really works. Why? Because this amazing truth about God's purposes for our bodies is not the only thing we need if we are to find a balanced and healthy approach.

REFRESHING REST

In order for us to find a healthy balance, we need to consider God's pattern of rest. At the very start of creation we see God create the universe in six days, but on the seventh day, he rested:

"And on the seventh day God finished his work that he had done, and he rested on the seventh day from all his work that he had done. So God blessed the seventh day and made it holy." (Genesis 2:2-3)

Isn't it interesting that the God of the universe, who doesn't grow weary or need sleep, chose to rest on the seventh day of creation? I'm so grateful that he did, because he was setting a pattern for us to follow (see Exodus 20:8-11). There are lots of debates about how exactly Christians should put Sabbath rest into practice today, but the principle is clear. We work hard, and then we rest. Unlike God, our bodies *do* grow weary—and that's ok!

After a long day caring for my family, or teaching a classroom of children, or working in the yard, my body literally aches for rest. I normally fall into bed at night exhausted—I'm asleep within minutes. That's what enables me to recharge for the next day. And we also need weekly rhythms of work and rest. Some people set aside Sunday as a day of rest and worship, but for us, being a ministry family often means that Sundays are especially full days. Even so, my husband and I have found setting aside one day a week for rest to be essential for the health of both our bodies and our marriage. Longevity in ministry will depend on how we care for our bodies. Simply put, we need refreshment in order to keep going!

It isn't just that, though. Choosing to rest from our work, or to go to sleep at night, is really an expression of trust in God. It's saying that you realize God will accomplish his will with or without you. As Psalm 127:1-2 reminds us:

"Unless the Lord builds the house,
   those who build it labor in vain.
Unless the Lord watches over the city,
   the watchman stays awake in vain.
It is in vain that you rise up early
   and go late to rest,
eating the bread of anxious toil;
   for he gives to his beloved sleep."

In our pride we can feel like we are the only person who can accomplish a certain task, or that needs won't be met without our endless sacrifice. We put it all on ourselves. We strive and strive. But God's purposes are way bigger than us as individuals—he doesn't need us. He is the one who will build the house or watch over the city! He's the one whose job it is, ultimately, to look after that person we're worried about, or to make sure we are able to put food on the table, or to grow his church.

It's not that we're not part of those endeavors: we are called to work. We're called to pour ourselves out for God's kingdom. But God also invites us to rest.

GIVING UP CONTROL

What do you imagine when you think of rest? For me, it means taking a break from work—shutting off my computer for the day and not looking at my emails anymore. It often looks like a long walk or a jog together with my husband. It can be dressing up for a dinner date, or doing a fun activity with the kids.

But I'm aware that to some, those things will sound like work, not rest! You long for a *break* from the kids. Doing exercise feels like a burden. The thought of dressing up to go out just piles on the pressure. So how do we decide what counts as rest? The question to ask is, "What's my motivation?" Am I doing this out of trust in God or am I striving? Is this a "have-to" or is it a "want-to"?

For some people, exercise is a refreshing break from a day of desk work. Others work their body hard every day, and rest will mean sitting on the sofa and watching a movie. Maybe you really enjoy clothes and makeup, and it's refreshing to you to pay a little extra attention to your appearance every now and then. Or maybe all of that fills you with dread, in which case you need to give yourself permission to chill out and just wear whatever's comfortable! Whatever your situation, and whatever is restful for you, it's about ceasing to strive, trusting God, and letting him be in control.[6] And this is something we can do every day, not just in planned rest periods.

My friend Ashley shared her story with me. "I've done all the things—counting my calories to within 20 points of my goal each day, counting every macro for every meal, exercising to the point of exhaustion—all because I had goals of what I wanted my body to look like. I thought if I could control every ounce of food that entered my mouth and do all the right exercises, it would yield the results that I wanted. In reality, I wasn't trusting God. I was living in fear of my body changing shape or size."

Does that chime with you? When we obsess over our appearance, it's often about control. We think that by strictly controlling our diet or adhering to a careful exercise regime, we can get the outcomes we want—not just the weight or physique we're aiming for, but the feeling of happiness or strength that we hope will come with it. We want to feel like we're in control of all things. We're like the person in the psalm, "eating the bread of anxious toil": we're forgetting that we can rest in God.

On the other side of the coin, apathy about our bodies often stems from striving so hard in other areas of life that we leave no time to care for our physical selves. Finding time to prepare healthy foods and exercise in the midst of life seems unrealistic. If we're honest, we've got caught up in doing too many things and we're failing to take the breaks we need. Again, we're seeking to control our lives; we're forgetting that we can trust God and rest.

Alternatively, bodily apathy may reveal an attitude of "giving up," of feeling like we have no control over our body. Maybe we've tried to lose weight, only to gain it all back and then some. Following all the rules and plans seems like a lost cause, so we don't bother even trying. Perhaps there is a sneaky whisper here saying to us that there's no point in trying to look after ourselves and be healthy because nobody even cares about us anyway, or because our lives don't make much of a difference to the world. But that isn't true. Body and soul, we are incredibly precious to God. We are temples of the Holy Spirit, called to glorify God for the long haul.

Our bodies were made to honor God. That means living his way, putting him first, and making sacrifices for the sake of others. But it also means resting, trusting, and taking care of the bodies he gave us.

A BALANCED PERSPECTIVE

In the remaining chapters, we're going to think through in detail what it means to honor God with our bodies in a variety of situations—and find freedom from our worries and struggles. As we do, it's important to remember that there are few black-and-white answers (outside the realm of blatant sin). Many of our choices are a matter of conscience and conviction: we will all practice the principles we've learned in different ways at different times, and that's fine!

For example: perhaps you are going to celebrate your anniversary with your husband. You'll likely make an effort with your appearance: fixing your hair, adding a touch of makeup, wearing an attractive outfit. That's great—it's right to honor your husband and the marriage vows you made before God. Enjoy it, and thank God for the body he gave you!

Now imagine that, the next day, you find out that another mom from church is battling the flu and needs some quick help with her young children. This is likely not the time to spend extra minutes in front of the mirror getting ready. In that situation, pulling on your sweats and putting your hair in a quick, unflattering ponytail can bring great honor to God.

Or let's say that the long-awaited weekend has finally arrived. Your kids are eager to spend time with you, anticipating your full attention and a fun family bike ride. Yet there's also a lengthy to-do list hanging over your head—the weeds need to be pulled, the house could use a good clean, and there are still those emails from work. What to do? Maybe you'll choose a couple of top priorities, give yourself a break from needing to finish the entire to-do list, and trust that the world will keep spinning even with dusty tabletops—and go on the bike ride. You honor the Lord by saving the energy you need for your most important relationships.

Another time, the work emails really won't wait. There's some kind of problem, and other people are going to be in trouble if you don't put some extra hours in. So you grab some fast food for everyone's dinner, turn on a favorite show or movie for the kids, and get the work done. It's ok that you're not being the Instagram-worthy "perfect mama" right now: it's honoring the Lord to serve your colleagues well, and your kids will be fine.

Consider exercise. One way to honor the Lord is to regularly get your heart pumping and work on strengthening your muscles, so that you're ready for whatever he calls you to do. It's what you need in order to be able to carry groceries inside for an elderly neighbor, help a friend pack up her apartment and move, or pick up young children. Yet there is also a time to forsake exercise. Maybe you're about to head to the gym when a friend calls who is desperate to talk something over. Honoring the Lord with your body here could mean staying put and offering a compassionate listening ear.

You might choose to honor God with your body by being careful about food. You eat the most nutritious food you can afford. You're attempting to steward your body well by how you fuel it! But then you're invited to dinner at the home of a friend who doesn't share the same convictions, or can't afford to buy the same quality of food. One way you might honor God with your body is to gladly and thankfully eat whatever is placed in front of you, trusting that God cares more about the state of your heart than the quality of your food.

In each of these examples, glorifying God means using our bodies to love others well. And it also means trusting that God is in control of all of it. We don't have to do everything! Even if we have to say "no" to an invitation to serve,

God can keep things going without us. Our security doesn't come through endless striving but through trusting that God loves us, regardless of the number on the scale or the checkmarks on our to-do list.

I wonder if you can think of a few examples of your own. Can you recognize ways that you're honoring God with the ways you use and treat your body? Or can you think of times when you now realize you were dishonoring God? Think about what you spend your time on and invest your money in. Ask the Spirit for discernment as you seek to find a healthy balance in your life.

A SPIRITUAL BATTLE

The world tells us all we need is willpower. I do my workout video and cringe at the self-help, positive talk the instructor gives. "How bad do you want this? You hold the power to change! It's all about your mindset." While there's some truth in the idea that our thoughts help determine our actions, the reality is that when we are fighting sin, we need something stronger to keep us on track than our own determination. Satan will use every means possible to keep our time and actions self-serving instead of God-glorifying.

The good news is that as believers in Christ, we're not thrust into this spiritual battle without divine help! God fills us with his Spirit and transforms us into Jesus' likeness. And he instructs us to put on the full armor of God so we can stand against the devil's schemes (Ephesians 6:11). In particular, we wield the promises and warnings of the Bible, the "sword of the Spirit," as our fuel to fight temptation. Immersing ourselves in the word of God changes our perspective on life. It changes our desires.

So, as we turn in the next few chapters to specific areas where many of us struggle to find balance—exercise, food restrictions, overeating, and aging—we are going to look to God's word and ask for God's help to honor him.

For now, next time you realize you are falling into the ditch of obsession or apathy, try remembering Psalm 16:11:

> *"You make known to me the path of life; in your presence there is fullness of joy; at your right hand are pleasures forevermore."*

Ultimate joy is found in the presence of God, not in losing 20 pounds or in gaining a sweet sensation in our mouths. When we shift our minds to an eternal perspective, the goals of our life change. And when we care for our bodies, use them for God's glory, and trust him with the results, that's when freedom is found.

FOR REFLECTION OR DISCUSSION

1. Do you feel like you have a healthy balance in your life with your body? Or do you identify with being a pendulum swinger? Which ditch do you tend toward— apathy or obsession? Why?

2. Read 1 Corinthians 6:19-20. Pause and consider these truths. What difference does it make to you that your body is a temple of the Holy Spirit?

3. What would refreshing rest look like in your life? How can you create times of refreshing rest in your schedule?

4. Our bodies are made to bring glory to God. Can you see the link between caring for our own bodies and being able to serve others well?

4. Buns of Steel

A BIBLICAL VIEW
ON EXERCISE

I have a favorite seat on the couch. My kids call it "Mom's spot." It's a cozy corner with a lamp for reading and an end table for my steaming cup of tea. It looks out through our living room windows at a towering oak tree in our front yard (and also provides the best angle for the television). I can get really comfortable in my favorite corner. So comfortable that sometimes, it's hard to motivate myself to get up off the couch to go for a walk or head to the gym—or even to clean up the shoes and socks off our living room floor. I've learned that sitting in that spot for too long will eventually make me tired and sluggish. My sedentary body just wants a nap! Whereas moving my body actually wakes me up and gives me energy. If I can push past the temptation to indulge in laziness, I'll be rewarded with a happier spirit and a more alert body.

Maybe you're in a different spot. You don't have any trouble getting off the couch to exercise, but sometimes, you can't seem to *stop* exercising. Just one more push-up, one more lap around the track. Missing a workout can feel crushing—like your day was ruined because you couldn't fit in your run. Or maybe it's hard to enjoy a good meal because you're contemplating how you're going to burn off the calories. Exercise doesn't feel like something life-giving but something controlling.

It seems like many exercise programs are built on the foundation of vanity, driving us to get into shape in order to create the best-looking version of YOU. They promise freedom from a negative body image, but end up enslaving us to their routines with the hope of sculpting the ideal body. I remember when I was a teenager looking at the cover of a popular workout video series entitled *Buns of Steel*. And yep, that was the goal. Your butt could be more muscular and attractive than the person next to you.

Of course, vanity isn't our only motivation for exercise. Some people exercise in order to gain physical strength or confidence in their bodies. And others are just trying to be the healthiest person they can be. Yet we have to be careful that even in our drive for "health," we're not being consumed with the wrong motivations, thinking we can control every aspect of our physical selves. It's a fact that God created our bodies to move. And strengthening our buns (and other parts of our body) certainly has value. Yet God purposed our bodies to move for reasons much bigger than staving off sickness or looking awesome in our bathing suits.

You might never have thought that God was interested in your fitness routine, but he is! So let's ask: what opportunities is God offering us here? What godly motivations does he provide? And no matter what our starting point is, how can the Bible help us find a healthier attitude toward movement and fitness?

IT'S NOT JUST YOUR BODY

"It's almost summertime, ladies! The shorts are getting shorter! Don't you want to be ready for the beach?"

"Hold that plank a little longer... you want to be sexy and strong!"

Over the years I've enjoyed various exercise classes at our local gym, but the barrage of self-focused motivations makes me cringe. Is this really what it's all about? Working out in order to have a beach-ready body? In order to feel good about ourselves in a bikini? No: we need to remember that as believers, it's not about us. And this is hugely liberating!

Contrary to what popular culture likes to tell us, as Christians our bodies are *not* our own. Like we saw in the previous chapter, they were bought with the precious blood of Jesus and now belong to God (1 Corinthians 6:19-20). And they house the third Person of the Godhead, the Holy Spirit. As temples of the Holy Spirit, we want to care for our bodies well, stewarding the earthly tent the Lord has given us. Romans 12:1 admonishes us:

"I appeal to you therefore, brothers, by the mercies of God, to present your bodies as a living sacrifice, holy and acceptable to God, which is your spiritual worship."

You might remember that the Old Testament sacrificial system required animal sacrifices—lambs or other animals without blemish were offered at the temple in order to take away the sin of the people. But since Christ came and paid the ultimate sacrifice with his life, we are covered in his righteousness, free from condemnation. Our body is acceptable to God because of the costly price Jesus paid. In contrast to all those dead animals, we are *living* sacrifices, meaning that we are alive from the dead—our sin being buried with Christ and our new life being raised with him (Romans 6:4). As followers of Christ, we offer our whole selves—our minds, the strength of our bodies, our words, our hearts—in order to bring glory to God. We may be striving for a more beautiful or strong or healthy physique, but our bodies carry so much more significance than just that: they can be instruments of praise to God!

Instead of offering an animal sacrifice in worship, we offer a sacrifice of praise—verbal accolades of God's greatness, despite the hardships we may be enduring. Our words remind us of God's faithfulness to his promises, his sovereign and loving care over our lives, and his mercy which calls us back when we've strayed. We please God by doing good with our hands—sharing what we have with others, or offering physical, tangible help to a friend in need (Hebrews 13:16). We readily sacrifice our own comfort and ease for the sake of another. In this way, our bodies are holy and acceptable to God. It's not an offering of bodily looks but bodily behavior. And it showcases the greatest purpose our bodies have on this earth—to point others to the living, all-powerful God. This is an act of worship.

Our bodies are all about God, not about us! Remembering this allows us to be free from the world's self-centered, never-satisfied motivations. It gives us a chance to reshape our whole perspective on exercise.

THE GREATEST RETURN

We can all worship God with our bodies, no matter who we are and no matter what we look like. But we are called to do this for the long haul, across our whole lives. That means that as we embrace this kingdom-minded perspective on our bodies, we need to think about how to care for them well.

Keeping our hearts pumping and our bodies strong will enable us to keep going, even as we age. Just as God gives us money to use wisely, relationships to invest in diligently, and time to use efficiently, so he gives us a body to steward well. God is the Creator of our bodies and entrusts us with their care. We make the most of this "earthly tent" which the Lord has given us by faithfully nourishing, moving, and resting our bodies (2 Corinthians 5:1). We discipline them in order to reap the greatest benefits from them.

Let's think about the parable of the talents in Matthew 25:14-30. In this story told by Jesus, a wealthy man going on a long journey entrusted his property to his servants, dividing it up unevenly:

> *"To one he gave five talents, to another two, to another one, to each according to his ability." (v 15)*

The man with the five talents immediately used it for trade and made an additional five talents. The man with two talents traded and made two more. But the man with one talent was afraid of the potential risks, and he went and buried the talent in the ground. When the master returned, he was pleased with the first two men, who had made a return on his investment. But the master was angry when he realized that the servant given one talent still only had one to give back. That servant operated out of fear instead of faith, hiding the talent and not working hard to make a return for his master.

The parable demonstrates that we must know and understand the character of our master in order to please him. The master expected that his servant wouldn't just hide and sit on his property, but that he would work hard to invest it and create more wealth. He was to steward—or manage and look after—the master's property, in hopes of gaining a fruitful return.

In a similar way, the Lord gives us a body to steward well. Your body is created and owned by a good God, hand-crafted just the way he intended. Whatever strengths and abilities he has granted you, he expects you to steward them well. You don't need to have the same productivity as others. The point is to use whatever you've been given to bring the maximum benefit to our good Master.

When we forget that our bodies are gifts to care for, we might be prone to give in to the fleshly desires of laziness or apathy, or (on the other end of the spectrum) bodily obsession. For those of us prone to excessive workouts, we need to discipline ourselves to rest, realizing that our bodies function best when they receive a break from constant activity. Maybe you ran an arduous course, and your legs and knees are feeling the after-effects the next day. Your muscles need time to rest and rejuvenate—it's probably not a good idea to push yourself to do another difficult workout. Remember that our righteousness is from the Lord, not from completing a certain number of hours of exercise or a certain distance covered! On the other side, some of us need extra encouragement to get up on our feet and push ourselves physically. Disciplining our legs to jog or our arms to lift weights or our hearts to pump hard creates a healthy body that's ready for action. Exercise keeps us fit, and this helps us to be faithful to God.

All of that sounds simple, but I know that when you're stuck in unhealthy patterns, it can be hard to get a clear view of what is healthy. You might want to steward your body well for God's glory, but still not know exactly how to do that. Should you go to the gym today or shouldn't you? Should you do that extra workout or something else instead? There aren't black-and-white rules! But the Bible does give us help to think through our motivations. I want to explore three specific ways in which exercise can help you and me to be part of building God's kingdom. If we have better motivations to focus on, we'll be able to find a better balance and a more God-centered perspective.[7]

1. READY FOR EVERY GOOD WORK

Jesus redeemed us from sin in order that we might be zealous for good works (Titus 2:14). And a life spent pouring ourselves out for the sake of others will come more easily with a strong and healthy body, right? In Titus 3:1 and 2 Timothy 2:21, Christians are exhorted to be "ready for every good work." We want to be available to serve wherever we're needed, with the energy and stamina the Lord provides.

We can use the strength of our arms to lift babies or children we care for, or to shovel snow for an elderly neighbor. We can use our legs to travel to places that need to hear the good news of Jesus, whether at your friend's house across the street or an unreached people group on the other side of the world. As pastor John Piper words it, we want to be "fit in order to be faithful"; we want to be "healthy in order to be helpful."[8]

I think of my friend Ellen, who in her fifties is diligent to exercise regularly, keeping her body strong as she helps her aging parents get to and from doctors' appointments. Her work as an occupational therapist is a physically demanding job—meeting with elderly patients who have had surgery or accidents, and teaching them basic life skills all over again. And I watch her on Sunday mornings, bringing a blind sister to church, helping her get in and out of the building safely. Ellen's diligent care of her own body enables her to keep serving a multitude of people. It's inspiring to see.

What about you? Can you think of ways that you've been able to serve others through having a strong and healthy body? Or maybe you're inspired to think of ways that you'd like to serve as you work diligently to get your body in shape. Remember, God is not unaware of the challenges that come with our physical selves. Your body doesn't have to look the same as another person's body or do the same things. But despite our differences, it's helpful for all of us to consider our opportunities to serve others as we decide when and how we exercise.

2. ABLE TO SHARE JESUS

The simple act of a regular workout routine opens the door to relationships you otherwise might not have. Personally, my usual gym session is tightly scheduled between school drop-offs, and I'm tempted to be laser-focused on accomplishing my goals, my own personal agenda. But when I'm willing to take my earbuds out, I get the pleasure of forming new relationships with neighbors pursuing a common goal. The gym has provided opportunities to befriend a young mom, offering a listening ear while on the treadmill and later dropping off a meal when her new baby arrived. I've even had opportunities to share my faith and invite a new friend to a Bible study—all while on the elliptical!

1 Peter 3:15 tells us, "Always [be] prepared to make a defense to anyone who asks you for a reason for the hope that is in you; yet do it with gentleness and respect." What does this look like for us? Maybe it could be a conversation as you gather for a Pilates class, or making the time to walk with a neighbor going through a difficult time. Unexpected spiritual conversations can happen when we keep our eyes and ears open to those around us.

The next time you're at the gym, ask God for courage to start a conversation with your neighbor on the treadmill. Show an interest in her life by asking about her day, her family, or her work. You might be surprised at the depth of relationship that can happen through simply sticking to a regular fitness routine, showing up around the same time on certain days. Relationships can sprout from asking another mom at school to be a regular walking companion, or initiating a conversation with the woman next to you in your Zumba class. And if we can be good friends to these neighbors, we can also look for chances to share the reason for our hope! So, I challenge you: ask the Lord to provide opportunities for new friendships the next time you go to work out—and be on the lookout for how he might answer your prayers.

3. HAPPY IN CHRIST

I've noticed on days that I get intentional exercise, my mind seems more alert. I can think through problems, articulate my words, and make sense of what I'm reading. When I start to get drowsy, getting up from my chair and doing a set of push-ups or crunches rouses my brain and body, allowing me to return to my work feeling refreshed.

But exercise doesn't just give me the ability to be more productive. I've also noticed that it provides an opportunity to grow spiritually. The promises of God seem more apparent and applicable when my mind has been awakened through exercise. Moving our bodies can help us continue to be students of God's word as we grow through regular study and meditation, unpack the promises of Scripture, and apply it all to our daily lives.

Famous evangelist and orphanage director George Müller once wrote:

> "The first great and primary business to which I ought to attend every day was, to have my soul happy in the Lord. The first thing to be concerned about was not, how much I might serve the Lord, how I might glorify the Lord; but how I might get my soul into a happy state, and how my inner man may be nourished."[9]

For some of us, getting our souls happy in Christ might mean we start our day with exercise in order to better focus on the truths of God's word. Why not try it: pray yourself out of bed and to the gym as a means of waking yourself up to ready your mind and heart for the intake of Scripture.

And that's not the only way in which exercise can make us happy in Christ. The stress that can result from difficult circumstances in our lives or the brokenness of the world around us can be consuming. Exercise can lift our eyes away from our own problems as we focus on working our bodies in a HIIT class or delight in God's beautiful creation as we jog through the park.

Personally, I exercise as much for the emotional benefits as for the physical benefits. Throughout my adult life, I've been prone to emotional highs and lows, and sometimes the lows are pretty deep. I've learned that as I keep the discipline of heading to the gym or going out for a jog, I'm rewarded with a happier spirit and an increase in energy. God often uses exercise as a means to turn my sullen mood toward a joyful one.[10]

And when my body is not dragging me down, I find it less difficult to delight myself in the Lord. Exercise has a way of clearing the cobwebs from my brain and helping to hold my focus on the promises of Scripture—so that I'm not just happier, but I'm happier *in him*. I am more ready to hear the sound of God's voice through Bible reading and meditation. I am more able to focus on memorizing a particular section of Scripture or on praying for the needs of those around me.

The next time you find yourself feeling blue, try moving your body as a way of lifting your eyes off of yourself and on to God. Could you combine exercise with prayer or Bible reading? Can you recite your memory verse while riding the stationary bike? Can you pray for your sister who is struggling in her marriage as you go for a walk? Can you simply notice the beauty of the world around you and take the opportunity to give God praise as you run? Try listening to worship music as you stretch or a Christian podcast as you lift weights. That way you get a double benefit: both a physical and a spiritual impact!

THANKFUL AND JOYFUL MOVEMENT

Seeing the opportunities that exercise gives us to honor God with our bodies can change our perspective. Before, we may have viewed exercise as a necessary evil or as an all-consuming demand, but now we can see it as a beautiful gift of God. We can thank God for our health and our ability to move our bodies, not taking it for granted that our limbs and muscles are working properly. We can remember all the ways God enables us to serve others through having a healthy body. As we change our mindset, exercise becomes a "get-to" instead of a "have-to."

This perspective change can also end up altering the choices we make with our exercise routine. I used to try to push myself to run a certain number of miles when I exercised. But I dreaded it. It was not fun or enjoyable because I was creating rules for myself. "You can't stop until you've finished 3.1 miles…" "You have to run at this pace, even if your body hurts…" "It doesn't matter that the weather is hot and humid today…" But as I've aged, I've realized that in order to keep exercising, I need to find movement that I really enjoy. So I've mixed up my workouts with stretching and strength-training classes, dancing, and lots of walking mixed with light jogging. As I move in these enjoyable ways, I have become more able to thank God for the gift of a healthy body to exercise—for arms that can lift weights, legs that can push bicycle pedals and lungs that can breathe in air. I thank him for the pleasure I feel when I move the body that he created. And I marvel at the creative ways I can both steward my body and delight in my Creator.

> *"Everything created by God is good, and nothing is to be rejected if it is received with thanksgiving, for it is made holy by the word of God and prayer."*
> *(1 Timothy 4:4-5)*

Do you feel that way about your body and the opportunities that you have to move and challenge it? Is exercise something that you enjoy? Something you look forward to? Or does it seem like one more thing you have to check off your to-do list?

No exercise will always be easy. It requires a push out of our comfort zones, and that's hard. But consider: is there something different you could do to help make movement more joyful? Perhaps there's a friend you can invite to the gym with you, or a favorite podcast you can listen to while you walk. Perhaps you could try a new sport, or maybe you just need to be less hard on yourself as you work out. Find whatever means the Lord provides to help you make the most of the gift of exercise. And pray that he will use it to make you happy in him, ready for every good work, and able to share the good news of his wonderful Son.

OUR SERVANT, NOT OUR MASTER

"Train yourself for godliness," Paul writes, "for while bodily training is of some value, godliness is of value in every way, as it holds promise for the present life and also for the life to come" (1 Timothy 4:7-8).

Some of us need to remind ourselves that exercise is valuable. We need to be pushed physically to get off the couch and get moving. At times, Christians can focus too much on the spiritual and neglect the physical. We can be so caught up in prayer meetings and Bible studies and evangelism that we forget the importance of caring for our own bodies.

But on the other hand, those of us who already love and enjoy exercise need to be reminded of what is paramount. Exercise is valuable, but only as it serves us in a greater mission—and if it rises to the place of master in our lives, then we've lost sight of what's most important. Our spiritual training should never take second place to our physical training. After all, our bodies on this earth will not last. No matter how much training we've done, no matter how many youth-enhancing procedures we've had, our bodies will weaken and fail. But our spiritual life impacts both the present day and the age to come. As Isaiah reminds us:

> "The grass withers, the flower fades, but the word of our God will stand forever." (Isaiah 40:8)

Whether you carve out 20 minutes each day, an hour or two each week, or much more than that, make a habit of fighting for joy in Christ through the habit of exercise. Regular exercise is worth so much more than achieving a smaller jeans size. It can be a pathway toward deeper love and joy in our heavenly Father—the one who stands forever.

FOR REFLECTION OR DISCUSSION

1. Do you exercise? Why or why not?

2. How might it change your perspective to view your body as a "living sacrifice" (Romans 12:1), or as a gift to steward well?

3. What are the three biblical motivations for exercise? Which is most helpful to you?

4. What is one change you will make as a result of reading this chapter?

5. You Are What You Eat?

A BIBLICAL VIEW ON FOOD RESTRICTIONS

I remember the first time I heard the popular mantra "food is fuel." I had recently taken up running (or slow trotting if I'm going to be totally honest) and was lamenting to a friend how hard it was for me. Did I mention I had never been a runner in my entire life? I still remember the dreaded "mile-run" in gym class—huffing and puffing, trying not to be in the last group of runners to finish. Give me dancing or kickboxing or bike riding, anything but running!

My friend, an avid runner, looked at me and said, "What are you fueling your body with?" She shared how once she changed her diet and started paying more attention to the foods she ate, running had become easier for her. I was hooked. What *was* I fueling my body with? Likely not the right stuff.

At the same time, another friend convinced me of a new diet plan that promised to shed pounds as easily as the skin off a snake. Of course, the plan only worked if you adhered to the strict regimen—my favorite baked goods and carb-loaded pizza were clearly off the menu. I was in my late thirties and realizing that the baby weight of child number four was sticking around longer than I'd like. I was open for suggestions. So I began my friend's healthy eating plan and the quest to find the best "fuel" for my body.

The only problem was, the regimented diet took all the fun (and taste) out of eating. I tried to convince my family that cottage cheese pancakes and zucchini lasagna were just as good as the real thing. But soon everyone groaned when they saw the familiar blue and white cookbook come down from the cupboard. "Not another Trim Healthy Mama recipe! Can't we have lasagna with real pasta?" they groaned.

It became apparent that I was the only one on board with the "food is fuel" mindset. Drinking my breakfast while everyone else sat down to pancakes and eggs didn't seem very fun. It felt like I was missing out—and my kids wanted me to enjoy the foods that they were eating together with them. "Aren't you going to have a waffle with us?" my daughter asked longingly. It reminded me of times when I've sat down on the couch and listened intently as my 9-year-old son showed me all his favorite baseball cards, even though I would never choose to look through baseball cards on my own time. There's something about delighting in things together that shows love to the people you're with.

There are a lot of different narratives being flung at us about what we should and shouldn't eat. It might be about fuel—figuring out what your body really needs and ditching everything else. It might be about weight loss. It might be about the impact our diet has on our skin or our gut or other aspects of our bodies. Some people have convictions about only eating food sourced in a natural or organic way, or not eating animal products. Some have medical conditions that demand particular diets. Others simply have a limited number of foods they really enjoy.

It's hard to sort through all this! You're probably asking: What should I prioritize? What do I do if the people I live with have different priorities? Which diet is *really* the best one? Which food is going to solve my problems? Before we know it, we can be caught up in spending hours researching diet plans or worrying about our weight. Or we feel overwhelmed by the responsibility to look after our health through what we eat—not to mention our children's health. Food suddenly becomes a big deal. It paralyzes us. Or, as I found, it stops us from enjoying time with those we love.

I should say at the outset of this chapter that there are some for whom this is a *really* big deal. A difficult relationship with food can develop into an eating disorder. These severe and complex difficulties can be life-threatening and need help from a doctor or a counselor—and I am not either of those! Here, my concern is for the many, many people who *don't* have an eating disorder but do spend a lot of mental energy thinking or worrying about food. (If you do fear that your worries about food may be starting to dominate you, turn to the appendix at the back of this book—among other things, it aims to help you start to think through what you may be experiencing and what the best next steps are.)

What I want to do in this chapter is to help you find freedom. We're going to hold up what our culture says about food restrictions against what the Bible says. And we'll find fresh perspectives that help us to worry less and enjoy food (and other people) more.

THE GOODNESS OF FOOD

First of all, we need to remind ourselves of the fact that food is a good gift from God. When God created food in the first chapter of Genesis, he created something from which we could gain both nourishment and enjoyment:

> *"God said, 'Behold, I have given you every plant*
> *yielding seed that is on the face of all the earth, and*
> *every tree with seed in its fruit. You shall have them*
> *for food ...' And God saw everything that he had*
> *made, and behold, it was very good."*
>
> *(Genesis 1:29, 31)*

God could have created one plant from which we would derive all our nutrients. Instead, he created a smorgasbord of flavors, textures, colors, and smells that our senses can delight in—the crunchiness of a nut, the sweet smell of oranges, the delicious taste of tender meat, and the brightness of leafy green lettuce.[11] Isn't God incredibly good in providing such richness? Even when you take into account allergies and intolerances, there is still something for each one of us to eat.

I find it striking how often in the Bible food is used to show God's steadfast goodness. Again and again he provides for his people. One of the most famous food stories in the Old Testament comes in Exodus 16, where we see God provide manna and quail for the Israelites. They are in the desert with no other food source, and God showers them with bread from heaven as his perfect provision. He tells them, "Then you shall know that I am the LORD" (v 12). The point is to show them who he is—a merciful God who provides for their every need.

Another time, God provides a suffering widow with abundant oil—not only enough to make bread for her and her sons but also enough to sell it on and pay off all their debts (2 Kings 4:1-7). And in passages like Isaiah 25:6-8, we find that rich, abundant, delicious food is used as a way of describing the glorious eternal life that God's people will one day have with him.

We see the same themes in the life of Jesus. He kept the party going at the wedding of Cana by turning water into wine (John 2:1-11). He miraculously provided enough food for the hungry crowds that followed him (Matthew 14:15-21). He used bread as a symbolic way to describe himself—"I am the bread of life"—pointing to the fact that he is the one who feeds, nourishes, and sustains us, both physically and spiritually (John 6:35). And he reinforced that point by choosing bread and wine as the symbols his followers would use to remember his sacrifice (Luke 22:14-20).

God cares about food. He knows we need it and he wants us to enjoy it—and through it, to enjoy *him*.

Do you see food as good? Maybe you feel guilty about enjoying particular foods. Maybe you worry so much about the impact of food that you *can't* enjoy it easily anymore. Maybe you have an intolerance that restricts your diet and you struggle with feeling angry or sad about everything you want to eat but can't.

Why not pause now and consider: what *is* good about food? What can I be grateful for, even in the midst of my frustrations or anxieties? Maybe you can think of a time when you really enjoyed food and saw God's goodness in it. Can you thank God for his good provision?

"YOU ARE WHAT YOU EAT": FOOD MORALITY

It's helpful to remember that, fundamentally, food is good. But this on its own doesn't solve all our difficulties around food or our worries about diet. What I want to do next is to delve into some of the things that can make food hard. Without realizing it, we can find ourselves swallowing narratives about food that change our attitudes and cause us to lose sight of God's good provision. The first of these is about food morality.

It's common to hear people give a moral value both to the foods they eat and to their behavior associated with the food. How often have you heard someone say, "I'm trying to be good today" as they pass on the plate of brownies? Or, "Oh, I've been so bad this week!" "Bad foods" are often associated with things high in saturated fat or sugar, and processed or convenience food—think chips, cookies, pop, fast food, and so on. "Good foods" are often considered those grown organically or non-GMO, plant-based foods or whole foods—fruits, vegetables, non-pasteurized milk, or grass-fed beef. Maybe you know people who say that certain diets are morally better because they have less environmental impact. Or you've seen mothers look down on each other because of what they put in their kids' lunches.

When we assign these moral labels to food, we become more susceptible to feeling false guilt or shame when eating. And the danger is that we begin to define our own morality by our menu choices. My teenage daughter once came home from school telling me about a friend who was distraught after eating a single Oreo cookie. "I am being so bad!" the friend had cried. "Why did I let myself eat that?" The cookie had ruined her clean-eating plan for the day—and she was despairing over what the processed sugar might do to her body. She wasn't able to enjoy a small treat because she was paralyzed by the thought of making a "bad" food choice. She felt like a bad person because of that one Oreo cookie.

Contrary to popular opinion, God desires for us to see *all* food, whether kale shakes or chocolate shakes, as a gift that can be received with thanksgiving:

> *"For everything created by God is good, and nothing is to be rejected if it is received with thanksgiving, for it is made holy by the word of God and prayer."*
> *(1 Timothy 4:4-5)*

The writer of that verse, Paul, is talking specifically about food restrictions. He is saying that no food is bad in itself. All foods—from a tangy lemon to a crunchy Dorito, from grass-fed steak to greasy sausages—are good gifts from God. And our diet choices *cannot* make us a good or bad person.

In the Old Testament, God did give the Israelites instructions regarding "clean" and "unclean" foods—not so different from our "good" and "bad" foods. Only certain "clean" animals were deemed appropriate to eat or offer as a sacrifice. This was part of God's design to show that his people were separate from the other nations. If you ate unclean foods, you were effectively turning away from God and counting yourself out of his people. So at that time, it was morally wrong to eat certain foods. But when Jesus came, he ushered in a new chapter of God's redemptive plans—and he did away with food morality.

There are two levels to this. One is that Jesus died for our sins. No matter what we have done, we are forgiven if we trust in him. Even when we have made genuinely bad choices, we can always find forgiveness and be made new. But the second level is that food carries no moral value anyway. You don't *need* to be forgiven for eating "bad" foods.

In Mark 7:15-22, Jesus clarifies the situation for us:

> "'*There is nothing outside a person that by going into him can defile him, but the things that come out of a person are what defile him … Do you not see that whatever goes into a person from outside cannot defile him, since it enters not his heart but his stomach, and is expelled?' (Thus he declared all foods clean). And he said, 'What comes out of a person is what defiles him. For from within, out of the heart of man, come evil thoughts, sexual immorality, theft, murder, adultery, coveting, wickedness, deceit, sensuality, envy, slander, pride, foolishness.'*"

Those are the things we need to repent of and find forgiveness for—our evil words, thoughts, and actions. Not our diets. This means there's no room to be proud because you have a "good" diet, nor to be cast down by shame because of your unhealthy habits. There's also no room to look down on others because of what they eat. You are free to eat what you want, and enjoy it—and so is the person over there who makes completely different choices than you.

GOD WELCOMES ALL

Even once we've been freed from the idea that food can make us a bad person, many of us will still choose to avoid certain foods. It might be a matter of personal taste or health, or it might be linked to some ethical issue—many people buy only fair-trade coffee, for example, while others reduce their meat intake for the sake of the climate. This chapter isn't the place for a full examination of all those issues! But I do want to say something about how we should relate to people who make different decisions than us about food.

In Romans 14, Paul writes to a group of believers who have differing views on food. Some want to enjoy meat that has been sacrificed in pagan temples, knowing that every food God has created is good and there is no moral obligation to avoid any of it. Yet there are others whose conscience tells them to avoid these foods that were formerly seen as "unclean." This disagreement is damaging their relationships (much as my over-zealous healthy eating began to damage my relationship with my family). In Romans 14:1-4, Paul helps them to see how to resolve this tension:

> *"As for the one who is weak in faith, welcome him, but not to quarrel over opinions. One person believes he may eat anything, while the weak person eats only vegetables. Let not the one who eats despise the one who abstains, and let not the one who abstains pass judgment on the one who eats, for God has welcomed him. Who are you to pass judgment on the servant of another? It is before his own master that he stands or falls. And he will be upheld, for the Lord is able to make him stand."*

Paul states that these choices with food are a matter of personal conscience. One person is not deemed more righteous or godly because of the restrictions they place on themselves, or don't place on themselves. Paul knows that no foods are unclean anymore, but he doesn't see it as a problem if some believers want to restrict their diets. The main thing is that it shouldn't get in the way of their fellowship with one another. God has welcomed both sets of believers, and so they in turn should prioritize their welcome of each other.

But do we actually live like that? This passage is calling us to be patient with those who restrict their food (or don't restrict their food) in ways we disagree with. Yet when we feel passionately about an issue, we can become blinded by our own thoughts and perceptions and lose sight of how to patiently welcome the other person.

To help, here are a few questions to ask yourself.

- When I'm deciding what to cook, do I put myself first or think of others?
- Do I judge other people's food choices, or am I willing to try the dishes others prefer?
- What tone of voice do I use to describe my food preferences or to talk about those who eat differently—do I sound haughty or do I empathize with others?
- How much time do I spend talking or thinking about food preferences, and how much time do I spend welcoming others through listening and focusing on them?

Thankfully, if we ask the Holy Spirit, he will help us to put aside our selfishness or judgmental thoughts and instead grow in love, joy, peace, patience, kindness, goodness, faithfulness, gentleness, and self-control (Galatians 5:19-23). He will help us to stop fixating on food dos and don'ts and instead welcome others—as Christ has welcomed us.

"CHOOSE HEALTHY, LIVE LONG": FOOD SALVATION

Wellness fads these days go far beyond simply restricting calorie intake in order to lose weight. Each new diet plan seems to involve a different combination of fasting and feasting or carbs and proteins, and promises us everything from greater energy levels to better appetite control, a happier digestive system, a lower chance of cancer, a more positive mood... The list goes on. It sometimes seems like what we eat can make or break us. If you make the right choices, the narrative goes, you'll be happy, healthy, attractive, and generally your best self. If you make the wrong choices, you're effectively consigning yourself (and those you cook for) to a life of unhealthiness, failure, and regret.

What we're being invited to believe is that particular diet choices will be able to solve all our problems. Not just our health but our whole experience of life will be transformed by eating the right foods. Diet can be our salvation.

This is a dangerous trap to fall into!

I'm not saying you should never follow a restricted diet. One or other of the claims I mentioned above may well be true—food clearly does have a big impact on us. And we can be grateful that God has created for us such a great variety of food that it is possible for one person to enjoy a completely different diet than another person! We're free to try out different eating regimes and see what helps.

But when we fall into the trap of believing that food can solve it all, we are effectively making it our god. And this is idolatry.

What problems are you hoping that diet will solve? What motivates you? Often, when we fall into idolatry, the desire we started with is actually a good desire that God can satisfy. Perhaps you avoid certain foods because of worries about your figure or other aspects of your appearance. You want to be attractive, because then you will be loved, respected, or admired. Can you remind yourself that God's love for you is already deeper than any human's could be (Ephesians 3:18-19)?

Perhaps you restrict your food because of health concerns. If a doctor has directed you toward particular foods or you have noticed that dropping some foods makes a notable difference to your health, that's great. But can you also make sure that you look to God to care for your body? Can you ask him to help you grow in trust of him, the one who has seen all your days beforehand (Psalm 139:16)?

Perhaps you pick your foods based on how they might alter your mood or your general sense of wellbeing. You want to feel good, be good, and impact those around you in a positive way. Can you make sure that you are also walking in step with the Spirit and asking God to work in and through you, and not depending solely on food and lifestyle choices? Can you trust him to lead you into paths of righteousness for his name's sake (Psalm 23:3)?

Perhaps you diet because it gives you a sense of control. When other aspects of life feel unpredictable or difficult, restricting food helps you feel you are on top of things. Can you remember that God knows your every need and is sovereignly watching over all your days (Matthew 6:30-32)?

Life is full of difficulties, and God doesn't promise to solve all our problems straight away. But he is at work in us, looking after us, and he promises to bring us to an eternity of joy and satisfaction. The world is full of lesser things which tempt us to worship them instead of him. But let's lean on our gracious, good Provider. If we restrict our foods, let's do so in a way that honors, instead of trying to replace, our God.

"HAVE IT YOUR WAY": FOOD INDIVIDUALISM

In Acts 10, Peter had a startling experience which he could not comprehend at first. The Lord was telling him to eat foods which he had always considered unclean. But now the Lord wanted Peter to disregard those Old Testament laws. Why? Well, we've already seen that Jesus declared all foods clean. But now we find out the effect that this declaration is supposed to have. Jewish Christians were now able to enjoy table fellowship with Gentile believers. Peter announced, "Truly I understand that God shows no partiality, but in every nation anyone who fears him and does what is right is acceptable to him" (Acts 10:34-35). The barrier between Jews and Gentiles was no more.

The kitchen table has a way of breaking down barriers between people—it has an amazing capacity to unite us. As we sip our coffee or eat our pie, an atmosphere is created in which we can share stories and get to know each other better. Even without eating together, a gift of homemade food to someone who is new to the area or in need of help and support can be a tremendous blessing to both giver and receiver. In my neighborhood, food provides opportunities for outreach as we host ice-cream socials in our backyard or hand out apple cider on Halloween.

And the Bible tells us that this breaking down of barriers is exactly what we are called to. In Christ, there is no partiality, and food is often the very best way of displaying that. As we said earlier, God wants us to enjoy food—and enjoy it *together*, even when there are profound differences between us.

Yet it's my experience—and maybe it's yours, too—that food restrictions can prevent us from enjoying the fellowship God intended.

My friend Lana was on a new diet to help her figure out what was causing inflammation in her body. There was a lengthy list of foods to avoid. Lana spent a significant amount of time preparing her food, as she normally couldn't eat anywhere other than home. At the same time, her husband decided that it was easier for him to drink a protein shake for dinner rather than prepare a separate meal that he could enjoyably eat. The end result? Lana and Steve stopped having meals together and were eating (or drinking) their premade meals whenever it was convenient. Lana confessed that their marriage was suffering. Previously dinner had been an opportunity to talk about the day and relax together, but now they spent that time apart.

Does this sound familiar? Lana and Steve had valid reasons for experimenting with food restrictions, but they found themselves isolated from each other. Our culture tells us to pursue the diet that works best for us, but the danger is that as our diets become overly individualized, we find ourselves divided instead of united. I don't just mean within one family. We can end up refusing invitations to eat with others at church because we're worried about what food they'll serve. Or we avoid inviting others for meals who we know have overly demanding diets. We can end up missing out on the glorious fellowship of believers that the gospel makes available to us.

As we decide which foods to pursue and which to avoid, let's make sure we are not falling into the trap of food individualism. Let's prioritize fellowship where we can. For example, when you go to someone else's place for a meal, consider how to be as low-maintenance as possible. For many people, if we're honest, our restrictions can be set aside for a few hours. Or if they can't—perhaps because of a medical diagnosis—we might offer to bring something we *can* eat or suggest a few recipes to make things easier for our hosts. It's a sacrifice to invite someone over for a meal; we should recognize this and be ready to eat gratefully and forego our preferences if we are able.

On the other side of the coin, we should also seek to be accommodating hosts—finding out others' requirements and catering for them generously. Sure, it might mean some extra preparation or expense, but if our goal is to make others feel loved and welcomed, we should be happy to go the extra mile. It's a small way of honoring others and serving them as Christ served us (Philippians 2:3-8).

A HOPE AND A PRAYER

One Easter Sunday years ago, I spotted a young woman sitting by herself in the sanctuary. After introducing myself and talking with her, I realized she was from out of town and without plans for the holiday afternoon. I was already hosting Easter dinner for our family plus a couple of other church families and decided to extend the invitation to the young woman. "We'd love for you to join us if you're free," I offered. She seemed hesitant in her reply: "Thank you but… I don't eat ham." "Well, I think we should still have plenty of sides," I said, hoping she'd still want to join us. But then she mentioned also avoiding dairy and gluten. As my menu ran through my head, I realized that I only had about two things she could eat. Still, I wanted her to feel welcome to join us. She accepted the invitation, and I ran home to whip up another side while my daughters quickly made another dessert that she could eat. My friend Jen graciously offered to grill a chicken breast at home before bringing her family over for dinner. Whew—I think we had it covered! 3pm rolled around, but as our guests arrived, the young woman was nowhere to be seen. About midway through dinner I received a text to say she'd decided not to come after all.

I don't know what stopped her coming. Was it embarrassment about her food restrictions? Fear that we wouldn't get it right? Maybe it was something else unrelated. But I was sorry that the story ended that way. It opened my eyes afresh to how paralyzing and limiting it can be to have so many worries about diet.

My prayer for you as you end this chapter is that you'll begin to feel free from this fear and guilt that can accompany food choices. As Christians, let's be known as people who enjoy the good gifts God has given us, whether that be grass-fed steak or Oreo cookies. And let's use the food God has given us as a means to show hospitality, to reach the lost, and to share the generous love of Christ.

FOR REFLECTION OR DISCUSSION

1. What popular narratives have you heard regarding food choices? How does the avalanche of information affect you?

2. Why do you think it is important to remember that food is fundamentally good? How might this affect the way you eat?

3. In what ways are you tempted to fall into the traps mentioned in this chapter (food morality, food salvation, food individualism)? What do you need to remind yourself of next time you are tempted to think in those ways?

4. What are some ways in which we can use food to welcome others?

6. The Chocolate Calf

A BIBLICAL VIEW ON OVERINDULGENCE

I love chocolate. I mean, really, really love it. I remember as a child going to Mackinaw Island in northern Michigan for vacation. Mackinaw is famous for its horse-drawn carriages (no cars are allowed on the island), bicycles that people ride around the perimeter of the island, and homemade fudge. A highlight of our trip each summer was walking into one of the many fudge shops and watching the workers spread the gooey chocolate out on a marble slab, shaping and forming it into the perfect fudge block. Samples abounded with as many varieties as you can imagine—peanut-butter chocolate, mint chocolate, cherry chocolate, just to name a few.

My two siblings and I always got to pick our own kind and carry it home in a white souvenir box. It was a contest to see who could make it last the longest (I always lost). My sister even went so far as to lick her entire block of fudge in front of me to keep me from secretly sampling it. She knew me well.

I still enjoy fudge. But at times I've also found myself rummaging desperately through the cupboards searching for even a hint of the stalest, cheapest chocolate—completely different to the rich, homemade fudge from Mackinaw. When there seems to be more work than hours in the day—the laundry pile is a mile high or the writing deadline is looming or the kids' schedules are leaving me exhausted—chocolate seems like a good remedy. I take my feelings to the nearest bag of chocolate chips. And I'm not satisfied with just a few: I keep needing one more handful until I realize that I'm not even enjoying the chocolate anymore. It's simply become a means of relieving stress through putting something sweet in my mouth. Maybe you can relate.

Overindulging in food is something that a lot of us struggle with. It can be an occasional thing that only rears its head when we're stressed, sad, or bored, or it can be a regular and life-defining issue. For some, it affects our weight and can therefore alter our self-esteem and sense of confidence.

By the way, it's also definitely possible to be a thin glutton! We can't assume that all thin people never overindulge with food, just like we can't assume all overweight people battle gluttony. Some people's weight is affected by the medication they take or a physical disability that prevents them from exercising. There are multiple reasons why a person's body is shaped the way it is.

For all of us, overindulgence can actually stop us from really enjoying and appreciating the food we have in front of us—you're not concentrating on that cool, sweet sensation of ice cream on your tongue because you're already thinking about the next scoop. It can also make our relationship with food complicated and guilt-filled, so that we swing back and forth between crash diets and overeating. (For a few, these complications become very deep-rooted and lead to an eating disorder. Do take a look at the appendix to this book if you need advice about disordered eating.)

An additional danger of becoming overly reliant on food is that it can pull us away from the God who gave it to us. You may not have thought of it this way, but overeating is not just a physical challenge: it's a matter of the heart. If we're only looking to ease our sorrows through a bag of chips or a bowl of ice cream, we've likely turned food into an idol. Anything we turn to first, apart from God, has the propensity to be idol worship. The experience of gratefully tasting the goodness of God through each mouthful of food is replaced by a cheap thrill of getting as much as you can as fast as you can.

Our culture is working against us here—especially in America. It wasn't until I was on an overseas study placement in Europe that I realized how enormous our food portions are in the United States. I walked to the corner ice-cream store with a friend and ordered a single, expecting the American-sized single of two giant scoops. Instead I got exactly what I ordered: one small, single scoop of ice cream on a cone. I remember thinking, "What?! This is all I get?" Many of us in the US have grown accustomed to super-size drinks, extra cheese on our pizzas, and ice-cream cones the size of our heads. Often it's actually easier to overindulge than it is to eat only the amount we really need! But large portions of food and access to whatever our desires crave are a dangerous recipe. They stop us from being self-controlled and appreciating what we have. We become focused on the greed of "more" instead of the gift of gratitude.

What about you? Are you a stress eater like me, or is your situation different? Maybe you've struggled with overindulging for many years—you'd like to have a healthier relationship to food but you're just not sure you ever can. Maybe overeating isn't a big issue for you at the moment, but you want to make sure you avoid it in the future. Maybe you eat pretty well in general, but there's one particular food or drink you just can't go without, and you're starting to think that's not helpful.

The aim of this chapter is not to give you a guilt trip with your food choices. Instead I want to bring you freedom and joy! How? By helping you to take these issues to the Lord. He is the one who made food for us, and he is the one who provides for us every day. He can help us have a positive and healthy relationship with food.

FOOD IS NOT THE ENEMY

I started the chapter by talking about comfort food. But it's important to say that taking comfort in food is not wrong. After all, didn't God give us food to enjoy and celebrate? We saw in chapter 5 that there is a myriad of feasts in the Bible! It isn't wrong to enjoy a bowl of steaming macaroni and cheese loaded with carbs and love, or your grandma's famous fried chicken, or a hot-fudge sundae shared with your honey after a stressful day at work. God tells us that he richly provides us with everything for our enjoyment—including leafy green salads *and* apple crisp:

*"As for the rich in this present age, charge them not to be haughty, nor to set their hopes on the uncertainty of riches, but on God, **who richly provides us with everything to enjoy.**"*

(1 Timothy 6:17, emphasis added)

There is something comforting about coming home after a long day to the smell of lasagna cooking, or pulling a pan of brownies out of the oven just as the kids get home from school—and that's good. Food is a gift to enjoy, no matter what the ingredient list includes. And God uses it as a means for us to show love and care for one another. "What's for dinner, Mom?" is a question I've heard often over the past 20 years of parenting. And I love when I can give an answer that spreads a smile across my child's face. It's satisfying to create a meal that my family enjoys eating together. Food is a comfort that can lift a weary heart. It is not the enemy!

But comfort foods *can* become gluttonous or sinful when they're the sole place we're looking for comfort. When we neglect time in God's word, or with friends, or in prayer, but we keep downing the bag of M&Ms in hopes of some stress relief.

Alternatively, we might treat food not as a source of comfort but as a reward. I was trained in this from the time I was a child. "Did you get a good report card? Let's go out for ice cream!" "Did you have a long day at school? Have some banana bread as a well done for working so hard." I've extended those rewards into adulthood—long day with the kids? I deserve a piece of cake. Finished my book deadline? Definitely a dinner out at my favorite restaurant.

Once again, food is not the enemy. It's great to enjoy a treat and to celebrate achievements and milestones. Yet, again, it starts to be a problem if this is the *only* way that you're rewarding yourself—when food becomes the primary way you can feel good about something you've done or the sole place you turn to help you cope when you've gone through something difficult. It becomes a problem when it starts to replace the comfort or the approval we can find in our God. This isn't about "bad" foods and "good" foods, or even the amount of food we're eating. It's about the heart.

THE GREAT PROVIDER

To find freedom from our heart issues, we need to reorient ourselves toward God. And our desire for food can actually help us to do so. How? Well, the fact that we need to keep refilling our bodies with nutrients is a reminder of our spiritual need. The Bible compares our need for God to a hunger for food or a thirst for water (e.g. Psalm 42:1-2). So, the rumble in our stomach can actively point us to the Giver of all good gifts (James 1:17).

After all, Jesus doesn't just provide food for his fickle followers. He himself is our food:

> *"I am the bread of life; whoever comes to me shall not hunger, and whoever believes in me shall never thirst." (John 6:35)*

Jesus is the source of our true satisfaction. He promises to quench the thirst of the God-shaped hole inside each one of us. Food is good, but it is not the main thing we need.

The Lord Jesus is. We need to remember this if we are to respond well to our cravings for more.

After the miraculous feeding of the 5,000, Jesus knew that the crowds were following to watch him create more sourdough and focaccia at the drop of a hat. We read in John 6 that they wanted their physical needs met. They wanted to see more miracles. They wanted more, even though they didn't necessarily need it! But Jesus exhorts them to incline their hearts toward heaven instead.

> *"Truly, truly, I say to you, you are seeking me, not because you saw signs, but because you ate your fill of the loaves. Do not work for the food that perishes, but for the food that endures to eternal life, which the Son of Man will give to you. For on him God the Father has set his seal." (John 6:26-27)*

Jesus himself is the sustenance we need for each day. Our endless pursuit of things on earth will fade away, and only what's done for the kingdom will last. Jesus is the provider for both our physical and spiritual needs. And it's only through him that we'll find satisfaction.

Next time you find yourself reaching for another helping or searching the cupboards for something sweet, can you pause and ask yourself what it is you're really after? Is it pleasure, comfort, reward, or just a distraction? Can you pray and ask God to provide for your needs *first*, before you turn to food? Can you thank God for the food he has given you, and savor the goodness of Jesus as you eat? Can you ask for his help in focusing on the food that endures to eternal life, instead of food that perishes?

TAMING OUR DESIRES

So, if our growling stomachs are meant to point us to Christ, what does that imply for our cravings on this earth? Is it sinful to go for that second slice of cake? As we discussed in chapter 5, there are no morally "bad" foods. Yet sometimes it can be hard to discern what counts as exercising our freedom in Christ and what is actually being sinfully overindulgent. Think back to the apostle Paul's exhortation:

> *"'All things are lawful for me,' but not all things are helpful. 'All things are lawful for me,' but I will not be dominated by anything. 'Food is meant for the stomach and the stomach for food'—and God will destroy both one and the other."*
>
> *(1 Corinthians 6:12-13)*

We have freedom in Christ to make different choices on these matters—as Paul acknowledges, "All things are lawful for me." But the point he then makes is that just because something is permissible, it doesn't mean that it's helpful in our Christian walk. Paul is warning us not to be dominated or enslaved by our appetites. Sure, I can eat steak, cookies, and chips without condemnation—but can I eat them with a grateful heart toward the Giver, recognize when I've had enough, and be content? Or do I know that I won't be able to stop?

This is where we have to cry out to the Holy Spirit for wisdom and self-control. If you know that eating one cookie will spiral you downwards toward eating the whole sleeve, then maybe it's best to forgo the treat. Or only eat it within the company of friends. One author words it this way:

> *"From time to time it's beneficial just to say no to your desires even if you are physically hungry for some particular food ... I must keep reminding myself that satisfying every whim of my body is self-serving, even if I do have Christian liberty. I relish my liberty in Christ, but I must keep my bodily desires in submission to my heart's desire to please God."* [12]

If we occasionally say no to a craving, we are reminding our bodies that we are not enslaved to that food. We can go without it and still be ok. As Paul says, we "will not be dominated by anything." If you find yourself feeling like you can't go without a certain food or drink, it might be time to say no to it from time to time. The point isn't that you're giving that thing up forever—it's just so that you know you can say no. Lean into the Lord's all-sufficient grace to give you the strength to walk the other way. He will help you build muscles of self-control and a greater dependence on him instead of on the food you desire.

This isn't about how much we weigh or what we look like. Whether we're eating a slice of cherry pie or choosing to forgo it, our ultimate goal remains the same—we eat and drink to the glory of God (1 Corinthians 10:31). We seek to honor God by how we think about our food, how we taste and chew and marvel at God's creativity. We aren't denying ourselves food for our own righteousness' sake or for reasons of self-regard, but to showcase the power of the Holy Spirit in our lives.

FIGHTING WITH FASTING

One way we can push against our sinful inclinations for "more" is with fasting.

I'm not talking about a crash diet here. Christian fasting isn't a way of losing weight but a way of losing our dependence on the world and growing in hunger for God. It has a spiritual goal, not a physical one. As John Piper says, "The root of Christian fasting is the hunger of homesickness for God."[13]

The western world is filled with pleasures that can seduce us away from the Lord. There's every kind of food you can imagine, available at the touch of a few buttons; there's endless entertainment—from TV and music to movies and plays. We're constantly tempted by lush vacations and bigger and better homes. When the concerns of the world start to consume our souls, so that we're constantly imagining the next best thing—whether that be the next meal, the next pay rise, a new house, or a different spouse—we've become a slave to our flesh. And the best way to fight that slavery is to replace it with a bigger, grander desire: a desire for God. He is greater than any of the things we're tempted by. Fasting is a way of reminding ourselves of that truth.

Let's say I fast from food. Whether it's for 24 hours or longer, or whether I'm just skipping a single meal and spending that time in prayer instead, fasting is a real test of my allegiances. Will I let my growling belly lead me to respond in anger—lashing out at others around me? Will I respond by caving to my desires? Or will I let my hunger remind me to pray, leading me deeper into my desire to put God first? When fasting is used properly, it reminds us where our true home is. The rumbling in our stomach at lunchtime jogs our memory of where our satisfaction comes from. It can sharpen our longing for God.

Fasting doesn't have to mean completely abstaining from food. In fact, it doesn't have to involve food at all. If you are someone who struggles with weight, it may in fact be unhelpful for you to fast from food: you'll likely end up focusing on the weight you're losing through not eating, instead of letting the fast lead you to a greater focus on God. Instead, you could try fasting from social media or coffee or watching TV—really anything you feel like you can't live without. Try it for an hour to begin with, or an afternoon, if more than that sounds daunting! The point is that we gradually grow in self-control in ways that end up spilling out over the rest of our lives.

While writing this chapter, I was convicted of my own lack of the practice of fasting. I've always had low blood-sugar issues, and skipping meals is not something my body can handle. But there are other ways that I can fast. Lately I've grown accustomed to having some form of dessert nearly every day—a cookie with the kids after school, a few chocolates when I walk by the staff workroom, a piece of pie with some friends we have over for dinner. I'm enjoying the truth that my freedom in Christ allows me to eat what I desire. But I've started to wonder whether my "freedom" to eat dessert has actually become a form of enslavement. Could I go without sweets for a day—or several days? Even though I can eat a brownie or cookie with a clear conscience, would I be able to forgo it when it was offered to me?

I want to desire the Lord more than a quick sugar fix, so I decided to fast from desserts for several days. I know this might not sound overly impressive, but for me, it was a real sacrifice! When those 3pm waves of weariness came that made me want to reach for a chocolate square, instead I shifted my focus heavenward and asked God to satisfy my cravings in himself—to sustain me with his strength. When the stress of a long day made me feel entitled to a treat, I asked God to help me love him more than warm brownies, and went outside for a walk. I want to remind my flesh that it's not in control of me—rather the Holy Spirit reigns in my body and my appetite. God is the one who gives me the strength to walk past the birthday treats in the office without a second glance, or to ride out the sugar craving with prayer for a greater hunger for him.

What about you? Is there a certain food or drink that you feel like you can't be without? Or are you medicating your sadness or anxiety with food? I encourage you to try a short fast and realign your perspective on food and your longing for the Lord. Let the rumblings of your stomach lead you to cry out in prayer and worship for the true bread from heaven.

A HIGHER DESIRE

Much of our gluttony is born of boredom—of being unsatisfied with life and indulging in food as our primary joy.[14] But there is one who satisfies us beyond any earthly pleasure. The greatest way to fight gluttony is to grow in gratitude for him.

It's no coincidence that God compares himself with food multiple times in the Bible. He is the bread of life (John 6:35), the manna we need every day. Think of Psalm 34:8, which exhorts us, "Taste and see that the LORD is good." He is the one who can fulfill all our deepest cravings.

We've talked about fasting, but how else do we fight the temptation to overindulge? We can spend time in God's word, memorizing and meditating on the beautiful promises of God. We can spend time in prayer, crying out to the one who loves to hear our voice, who loves for us to lean into him. We can spend time enjoying the gifts he has given us—the beauty of trees and music, the joy of spending time together, the satisfaction of work that brings glory to him.

We can also enjoy the gift of fellowship in the local church. What better way to fight our sin than to join arms with fellow brothers and sisters in Christ who can hold us accountable, bear our burdens with us, and exhort us to find our fulfillment in Christ? The body of Christ is a gift that we shouldn't take for granted. If you think you need help with battling overindulgence, could you share your struggles with just one or two trusted Christian friends who can pray for and encourage you?

Before I close, I want to say a word to those who feel deeply ashamed of their lack of self-control with food. Friend, even when you've blown it, even when your best efforts have failed, you can rejoice in the truth that there is no condemnation for those who are in Christ (Romans 8:1). Jesus died for our past, present, and future sins. We don't need to walk around with a cloud of guilt over our heads. Instead we can remember that his mercies are new every morning—or as I've heard it said, his mercies are new with every *meal*.

Trust that the Lord is for you and not against you, and lean into his merciful, gracious arms to receive forgiveness. And when you're tempted to overindulge, bank the promise of 1 Corinthians 10:13—that no temptation has overtaken you that nobody else has experienced before. God is faithful, he knows your heart, and he will provide help to escape sinful desires.

When the good gift of food threatens to become too important in our lives, let's remind ourselves of the gracious and generous call of God:

> *"Come, everyone who thirsts,*
> *come to the waters;*
> *and he who has no money,*
> *come, buy and eat!*
> *Come, buy wine and milk*
> *without money and without price.*
> *Why do you spend your money for that which is not bread,*
> *and your labor for that which does not satisfy?*
> *Listen diligently to me, and eat what is good,*
> *and delight yourselves in rich food."*
>
> *(Isaiah 55:1-2)*

Our Creator God is the one who can satisfy us, far more than the tastiest pasta or the sweetest wine. God's invitation turns us away from the fading pleasures of the earth and reminds us that *he* is the richest gift—one we can savor and enjoy all the days of our lives.

FOR REFLECTION OR DISCUSSION

1. What causes us to indulge with too much food?

2. Why is it spiritually dangerous to become overly reliant on food?

3. How can we enjoy food in a God-honoring way?

4. How do we fight the temptation toward gluttony?

7. Laughing at the Days to Come

A BIBLICAL VIEW ON BEAUTY AND AGING

For hundreds of years our culture has been obsessed with youth. In elementary school I remember learning about the 16th-century Spanish explorer Ponce de Leon, who supposedly went in search of water that would keep him young forever. The well he is said to have found is now known as the Fountain of Youth and is the oldest tourist attraction in Florida, with guestbooks dating back to 1868. Visitors can still taste the sulfur-smelling water in hopes of curing illness and turning back the hands of time.

This ideal of eternal youth has not changed—although it has had an update. Anti-aging campaigns in today's beauty industry offer everything from miraculous moisturizers that promise to erase wrinkles to pricey injectable fillers like Botox. The latest diet fads promise to add years to your life and give you the energy of a teenager. The fitness industry pushes us to work out to achieve the body of someone ten years younger—your "best self" being one without wrinkles, a sagging waistline, or any signs of wear and tear.

With the immense pressure to stay looking youthful and fresh, our culture is sending a message: stop aging at all costs! When we try to disguise our age by veiling our faces and bodies in cosmetic procedures, we're buying in to the message that our value lies in our appearance. A friend of mine in law enforcement told me that she thinks cosmetic procedures and surgeries are fueled by the epidemic of pornography. Women feel like they're being compared to the unattainable, filtered images online and are deceived into thinking that they have to keep up.

Actress and author Justine Bateman has become known in Hollywood for her courage to age naturally. After seeing pictures of herself online tagged with comments that she looked old, Bateman became ashamed and self-conscious of the lines on her face. She realized that the obsession to look younger is fueled by fear:

> "I think that everybody has a completion to this sentence: 'I'm afraid if people think I look old then therefore _____,' and for different people it's different things. Some are afraid they'll lose their job or never get a job or not get a mate or no one's going to listen to them or whatever. My position is, that fear existed before your face started changing … I'm just somebody who got myself on the other side of what that fear was for me in particular."[15]

Bateman is onto something. As I was preparing to write this chapter, I sent out a survey on aging to a wide spectrum of women in various stages of life. Although no one gave exactly the same answers, I noticed a trend of fear. One friend commented that though she doesn't fear the natural wrinkles that may form on her face, she fears losing the physical capabilities that she has now. She and her family have always been active people who love sports and the outdoors. It can be hard to imagine enjoying life with a loss of physical movement. Another friend shared the fear of losing her physical attractiveness. "Society has trained me to think that if I don't keep up my appearance, if I don't stay thin enough, my husband will stray and be unfaithful." A third woman shared the fear of succumbing to the same disease her mom had: "It can be hard not to fear the worst and expect that I'll get Alzheimer's. I worry about my husband and how he'll handle caring for me. I worry about my kids. I know God is sovereign over all of life, but it can be hard to trust him with the future."

Maybe you're at a point in life where aging isn't even something that you think about. You're busy with your career or taking care of young kids. Or maybe you're at a spot, like me, where nearly every day there seems to be a new gray hair that's popped up, or a new line on your face. In a culture obsessed with youth and beauty, it can be hard to keep a proper perspective on aging. Let's take a break from social media, filtered images of famous women, and all those anti-aging commercials, and consider aging from an upside-down, kingdom-minded perspective.

A CROWN OF GLORY

Here is how the Bible celebrates the growing number of candles on our birthday cake:

"Wisdom is with the aged, and understanding in length of days." (Job 12:12)

"Gray hair is a crown of glory; it is gained in a righteous life." (Proverbs 16:31)

"The righteous flourish like the palm tree, and grow like a cedar in Lebanon ... They still bear fruit in old age; they are ever full of sap and green."
(Psalm 92:12-14)

I love the picture these verses create in my mind: a joyful woman with gray hair, spiritually strong, full of wisdom, and still bearing the fruit of service to others. But it's countercultural: when was the last time you thought of the gray hairs on your head as a *crown?!*

The idea here is that gray hairs are gained through living a righteous life. These verses take our minds off our appearance and all the fears that go with it, and redirect our attention to our *spiritual* maturity instead. Suddenly it becomes possible to celebrate becoming older, because we are seeing how God has shaped us over many years.

It's pretty much the opposite of our culture's view of aging. But do you see what the Bible is getting at? The longer we are on this earth, the more opportunities we have had to trust Jesus and grow in wisdom. We've experienced more ups and downs and have a perspective that spans decades of life. All of the trials we've walked through— singleness, financial loss, raising children, chronic illness, bereavement—have been used to shape who we are. Those things might not have been easy, but God has been there with us in them. And changes to our physical bodies can serve as a reminder of that.

How about you? Leaving aside your fears about the future for a moment, can you look back at your past? Can you see how you've grown in spiritual maturity—whether you've known Jesus your whole life or just for a short time? Can you see how you've grown in the fruit of the Spirit—love, joy, peace, patience, and so on (Galatians 5:22-23)?

Next time you look in the mirror and notice all the ways your body has changed, try looking at it in a different way. Those stretch marks and loose skin around your abdomen—maybe they're a reminder of the gift of children. Those dark circles under your eyes—perhaps they show the late nights you've spent counseling a troubled friend or anxious teen. That furrowed brow reveals the hard trials you've worked through trying to figure out how to be a good friend or family member or a diligent worker. Those crow's feet and laugh lines are sweet reminders of good times spent delighting with friends and family.

The physical signs of aging are not marks to despise, but signs of how the Lord has worked through your circumstances to turn you into the person you are today. And therefore they are signs of how you can trust him for your future, whatever your fears.

A FLOURISHING FUTURE

As we look to the future, we can pray that we'll be like the flourishing palm tree of Psalm 92—still bearing fruit in old age, still green and full of sap. Yet I'm aware that some will be reading this and thinking, "But I'm not righteous. I'm not like that tree. The lines on my face just show how *badly* I've lived my life. All those mistakes. All those wrong turnings."

Can you trust that the Lord who loves you can make you righteous? I quoted verses 12 and 14 of Psalm 92 above, but in between comes verse 13:

> *"They are planted in the house of the LORD; they flourish in the courts of our God."*

If we want to flourish in our older age, we need to be planted in the house of the Lord. It's Jesus' righteousness we depend on: it's when we put our faith in him that we are able to flourish. We lean into his word for wisdom, counseling our own hearts not with the advice of this age but with the unfailing truths of Scripture. We spend time in prayer, asking him to guide and sustain us. We serve others and live lives of righteousness because he is our example and our enabler. Even when we have lived a life full of mistakes, sins, or sufferings, our Lord can turn them for good and shape us into his likeness (Romans 8:28; 2 Corinthians 3:18). Whoever we are, it's because of Jesus that we can start to experience gray hair as a crown.

But what does this flourishing righteousness actually look like? I think of a few beautiful older women in my church, like Sharon, who has spent many of her retirement years mentoring younger women, teaching Bible studies, and caring for her aging parents in her home. I think of Denise, who spends a majority of her week sacrificially caring for her two grandchildren while their parents are at work. I think of Jan and Sally, who provide childcare at our moms' group so that younger, exhausted moms can have a couple of hours to enjoy fellowship, coffee, cake, and biblical encouragement without their littles. These women are bearing fruit because they are looking to Jesus, their Lord and Savior, each day.

Each of these women offers a sterling example of what is described in Titus 2:2-5:

> *"Older men are to be sober-minded, dignified, self-controlled, sound in faith, in love, and in steadfastness. Older women likewise are to be reverent in behavior, not slanderers or slaves to much wine. They are to teach what is good, and so train the young women to love their husbands and children, to be self-controlled, pure, working at home, kind, and submissive to their own husbands, that the word of God may not be reviled."*

This passage highlights the wisdom, grace, and steadfastness found in godly older saints, calling both older men and older women to be living examples of a righteous life and to train the younger men and women behind them. They are to be a model of good works, showing integrity, dignity, and sound speech in their teaching.

How can you and I be Titus 2 women? We can put the gospel on display through delighting in our husbands and children (v 4), not seeing them as burdens but as gifts from the Lord. By modeling self-control with our words, appetites, and behavior (v 5), we can provide a godly example for the younger generation to follow (v 4). Our purity (v 5) will shine as we seek to honor Christ with our eyes, our lips, and our bodies, trusting that Jesus will enable us to do so. We can work hard to make our homes a place of refuge for all who enter, showering kindness on both the everyday household members and the guests who walk through our front doors. And contrary to so many attitudes toward marriage in our culture, Titus 2 women can honor their husbands with a respectful demeanor, not seeking to dominate him nor being controlled by him but looking to him as the leader of their homes (v 5; see Ephesians 5:21-33). All these actions are dependent on the grace of God to work in and through us as we trust in Jesus.

THE LONG VIEW

As believers in Christ, we can rejoice that the Lord has given us the years to be Titus 2 women to the next generation. I've said that this depends on Jesus working righteousness within us, but Titus 2 also mentions another factor that is crucial for helping us to see our gray hairs as a crown of glory: the hope of heaven.

> *"For the grace of God has appeared, bringing salvation for all people, training us to renounce ungodliness and worldly passions, and to live self-controlled, upright, and godly lives in the present age, **waiting for our blessed hope,** the appearing of the glory of our great God and Savior Jesus Christ."*
> *(Titus 2:11-13, emphasis added)*

These verses remind us of the big picture of how God is working, and invite us into a "long view" of life. We pursue living a life of righteousness, being zealous for good works, because of the hope we have in Jesus. He is coming back, and we want to be ready. When we think like that, the wrinkles around our eyes don't seem to matter very much anymore! The hope of heaven lifts our eyes off ourselves and our present circumstances and onto eternity.

Yet sometimes having a long view of life is challenging to attain. When we're drowning in the daily trials of life, or fearful for the future, or feeling jealous or discontent, it's easier said than done. So I want to take some time to consider an older woman in the Bible who struggled with just those feelings.

Naomi was no stranger to suffering. The first chapter of the book of Ruth tells us of a famine which had driven Naomi's family to move away from their homeland of Judah to the foreign country of Moab in hopes of finding food. After a difficult move and struggling to feed her family, further disaster struck: Naomi's husband, Elimelech, died. She was left as a single mother of two boys, who then married foreign wives, Orpah and Ruth. After ten years, both Naomi's sons died, so that she was left only with her two daughters-in-law.

Naomi must have felt left behind, washed up, past it. For her, it wasn't that potential employers might not take her seriously because of her gray hair, or her husband might not find her attractive anymore because of her aging body. Naomi had no husband. She had no future—at least, that was what she thought. We see her saying to her daughters-in-law, "I am too old to have a husband" (Ruth 1:12)—and by implication too old to have more children, a big deal in her society.

Did she fear not being provided for? Struggling to have food and the basic necessities of life? Maybe she was sad that she would not leave behind a legacy—she seemed to have lost her chance to have grandchildren and pass on her faith to another generation. Either way, after this barrage of disappointments, Naomi had no hope. And as she grieved her difficult circumstances, she blamed God for her lot:

> *"The Almighty has dealt very bitterly with me. I went away full, and the LORD has brought me back empty." (Ruth 1:20-21)*

Is this you? Maybe you feel bitter, like Naomi, about everything that has happened to you. As you look to the future it feels bleak and not hopeful.

Maybe you're still young, but you fear the future even so. As your first wrinkles appear or your body starts to seem less resilient than it was, you wish you had made more of your youth and you worry that it's all downhill from here. Maybe you find yourself looking in the mirror and wondering where things went wrong. Or maybe you think, "Other people age gracefully, but that can never be me."

But the story of Naomi teaches us: don't write yourself off!

Naomi was blinded by her difficult circumstances. She only saw her losses in life and forgot to notice that, in fact, God was still working in the midst of her pain. Despite Naomi's anger at God, he met her with mercy and grace.

First Ruth, her daughter-in-law, showed a remarkable display of *hesed*, steadfast love, to Naomi by sticking beside her all the way back to Bethlehem. Then Ruth met Boaz, a relative of Naomi's husband, who kindly let Ruth glean grain in his field, providing more than enough food for both women. Finally, Boaz agreed to marry Ruth through the laws of redemption.

And it wasn't just that. Boaz "redeemed" Ruth, but ultimately he redeemed Naomi's story as well. Ruth became pregnant with a baby boy, Obed. At the end of the book of Ruth we see the women praising God for what he did in Naomi's life:

> *"Blessed be the LORD, who has not left you this day without a redeemer, and may his name be renowned in Israel! He shall be to you a restorer of life and a nourisher of your old age." (Ruth 4:14-15)*

The women see that God has provided a future for Naomi. Boaz and Ruth were providing for her present, but little Obed would be the one to nourish Naomi in her old age. For the rest of her life, she would have love, belonging, a home, a family—in other words, all those things she probably feared she had lost forever. What was more, Obed was the father of Jesse, the grandfather of David, in the line of Christ (Ruth 4:17; Matthew 1). And Jesus Christ is the redeemer of all God's people. Naomi's story would be forever part of the incredible storyline of salvation.

That's the long view of Naomi's life. And although she lived in very different times, the long view is not so different for you and me. Despite our worries, we can face the future with confidence, not bitterness, because we face it with God.

LIFT YOUR EYES

Sitting next to my friend, I noticed a small bruise under her eye. I waited for a time when we were alone to ask what happened. "Oh," she said, "it's just a bruise from Botox. Injecting the needles can break your blood capillaries. It should fade away soon. It hurt like crazy!" My friend explained how her sister, a nurse, offered her a free Botox treatment in the privacy of her own home. "When you're 41 and have 3 kids, it's pretty hard to refuse." I understood how she felt!

My friend went on to explain how her sister is raking in the dough doing "Botox parties." Women gather in groups of friends to enjoy martinis, music, and Botox injections. It's become a group celebration. Yet when I started to research Botox, I discovered hundreds of stories of treatments gone wrong. Eyebrows completely frozen in place for months, a lip that swelled to the point of needing to go to the emergency room, and side effects that include blurred vision and headaches.

There's an irony in spending an endless amount of money, time, and pain on beauty treatments that can leave you looking worse than before. Needles injected into your face that can offer both smoother skin and a black eye. Yet in America and many other countries, this has become a common experience of life. Even my hairstylist, Jordan, who is in her mid-twenties, told me of her twenty-something friends who are already hooked on treatments. "Once you start, you can't stop. You have to keep up the same look, with a downward spiral of money and time."

Does that sound at all familiar? Maybe for you it isn't Botox. Maybe you spend money on serums and creams, or hair dye. Maybe you work harder and harder to keep fit and flexible as you get older. Maybe it's the latest diet fad, buying special nutrient foods in hopes of losing a few pounds. Whatever it is, do you perceive a "downward spiral of money and time" in your own life?

Let me be clear: it's good to enjoy and make the most of the bodies God gave us. Caring for our physical bodies is a good thing, and this may include beauty or anti-aging treatments. Yet we do want to be able to make wise and godly decisions that honor God rather than just jumping on the cultural bandwagon. So, while I'm not going to give you a list of dos and don'ts, I do want to give you a few questions to consider before moving forward with beauty decisions.

- Why do I want to do this? What is my heart behind wanting smoother skin or a different color for my hair?
- What is the fear lurking behind the desire to look younger? Am I fearing man or God?
- What would it look like to trust God with my fears?
- Does this product or procedure have any inherent risk to my health? Is it safe?
- Do I have the financial resources to afford this without sacrificing something more important?
- What am I teaching my daughters or other women around me by my decisions?

I'm reminded of this favorite passage in 2 Corinthians 4:16-18:

> "So we do not lose heart. Though our outer self
> is wasting away, our inner self is being renewed
> day by day. For this light momentary affliction is
> preparing for us an eternal weight of glory beyond all
> comparison, as we look not to the things that are seen

*but to the things that are unseen. For the things that
are seen are transient, but the things that are unseen
are eternal."*

As believers in Christ, we are called to have a mindset that
is opposite to the world's. We're called to look beyond what
the eyes can see and what the hands can touch, and to
remember that the Lord longs to nourish and strengthen
us. He longs for us to look beyond our wrinkles and bodily
changes and keep our eyes on him. The weightiness of the
trials of life and our fear of aging pale in comparison to the
riches of eternity.

A purely temporal view focuses on the extra pounds you
gained when you were pregnant with your children. But the
eternal view reminds you of the gift of children to raise, and
the opportunity to pass on your faith to the next generation.

The temporal view fears the loss of physical beauty as a
new gray hair pops through. But the eternal view focuses
on the lessons learned and wisdom gleaned through living a
full life, and how you can pass it on to others.

The temporal view obsesses over erasing the laugh lines
and crow's feet on your face. But the eternal view rejoices in
the well-earned reminders of laughter with your loved ones.

The temporal view fears losing physical ability and being
dependent on others as you age. But the eternal view
reminds us that when you're weak, you're strong, as you
lean into the heavenly Father for strength for each day.

LAUGHING AT THE TIME TO COME

As we courageously move forward in our lives, fighting the
fear of aging with truths from God's word, we will grow to

be like one of the most revered women in Scripture. The Proverbs 31 woman can seem a bit daunting to the average person. She is the apple of her husband's eye and adored by her children. She diligently watches over the affairs of her household. She is a businesswoman, making wise investments and earning income for her family. *And* she generously gives to the poor and needy around her. But the quality that I admire most about the Proverbs 31 woman is her lack of fear for the future:

> *"Strength and dignity are her clothing, and she laughs at the time to come." (Proverbs 31:25)*

The Proverbs 31 woman is not concerned about her aging face, or about losing her faculties as she gets older. Instead, she is clothed in confidence from the Lord as she "laughs at the time to come."

How would our world be different if Christian women didn't fall into the traps of the world, but instead shone like this woman, like beacons of hope in the night? If we didn't chase youth and physical beauty, but instead accepted our creases and our added pounds as a God-given part of life? If we didn't fear the future but exemplified a rich trust in the sovereignty of God?

My friend Andi shared a sweet story about her mom at a Bible study recently. "My mom was a beautiful woman. Even though my dad was a difficult man to be married to, my mom always responded with gentleness and grace. When I wrote her obituary, I listed the fruits of the Spirit— because that list described who she was. She was the only Bible some people would ever know." Andi's mom's beauty didn't come from products or procedures, but from knowing and living out the word of God. She was a testimony of God's grace for all who knew her, a shining star in a dark world.

The gospel is good news for aging, ladies. Despite the added candles to our birthday cakes, we will grow more beautiful as we grow more like Christ.

FOR REFLECTION OR DISCUSSION

1. Why is our culture obsessed with youth and beauty? Do you resonate with any of the fears about aging that were mentioned in the chapter?

2. How does the Bible's view of aging compare with the world's view of aging? Which of the truths in the sections "A Crown of Glory" and "A Flourishing Future" did you especially need to hear?

3. Do you know any Titus 2 women in your life? How do they exemplify flourishing in righteousness (Psalm 92:13)?

4. What are some practical ways we can assess our decisions in terms of beauty products and procedures? How can we fight to have the "long view" of life?

Conclusion

L earning to see my body as a good gift from God has been a process. And retraining my mind to think about my appearance, food, and fitness from a biblical perspective is still a work in progress! Our fallen world does not make us naturally wired to be grateful for who God made us to be or to put his purposes first. And in modern Western culture we're constantly pushed to focus on our imperfections. But God, in his goodness, invites us to trust him with all our bodily concerns. He desires us to walk in both freedom and joy, casting on him each burden that plagues our minds. He tells us, "My yoke is easy and my burden is light" (Matthew 11:28-30).

Through Christ's death on the cross and his resurrection, he has freed all those who follow him from the power of sin and death. He's freed us from the heavy chains of insecurity, discontentment, food rules and addictions, compulsive exercise, and disordered eating. As Paul reminds us in the book of Galatians:

"For you were called to freedom, brothers. Only do not use your freedom as an opportunity for the flesh, but through love serve one another." (Galatians 5:13)

In our newfound freedom we can use our bodies to bring glory to God. Instead of obsessing over our physical appearance or being apathetic, we can lean into the Lord for godly wisdom and self-discipline. We can look for ways to be thankful for how God created us (no matter how many lines are on our faces!), and we can care for our physical selves in a way that enables us to serve others. The efforts we make to strengthen our muscles, to rest, to eat nourishing foods, to offer hospitality, and to forgo our preferences for the sake of others can all be signs of the Spirit of God dwelling inside of us.

So what about you? As you finish this book, what have you learned? What changes have you started to observe in your own attitude already, and how has it impacted your experience of food, exercise, and life in general? What areas of concern do you see in your life that you want the Lord's help with, and in what ways are you already in a good place, with a balanced view of your appearance, fitness, or food? Consider: what insight from Scripture do you want to make sure you don't forget, and how can you make sure you remember it? And as you look to the future and to those around you, is there anyone else you could help to find a pathway to freedom?

Wherever you're at in this journey of life, know that you're not alone. God loves for us to cry out to him for help. He is our faithful high priest, able to sympathize with our weaknesses and ready to give us the grace that we need

(Hebrews 4:15-16). And he is more than able to help us walk in freedom. God doesn't leave us to fend for ourselves but equips us with his Spirit and the promises of his word to spur us onward.

Here's one of those promises to leave you with:

> *"I am the bread of life; whoever comes to me shall not hunger, and whoever believes in me shall never thirst." (John 6:35)*

No matter what your reflection in the mirror looks like, your truest joy and satisfaction comes from the Lord. He is the one who will satisfy you, far more than a decadent dessert or an ageless complexion. So let your hunger be satisfied and your thirst quenched through Christ alone. As we lift our eyes off of ourselves and onto the Lord, we'll be more and more transformed into his image—where we can walk in beautiful freedom.

Appendix

THE RED FLAGS OF
DISORDERED EATING

It's possible that, as you have read this book, you are beginning to wonder if you've developed some unhealthy eating or exercise patterns in your life. Maybe the chapter on food restrictions made you question your true motivations for your diet plan. Maybe the chapter on overindulgence highlighted an unhealthy over-reliance on food. Or maybe you're thinking of someone close to you—a daughter, sister, or friend who you fear might be enslaved to compulsive exercise, strict diets, or deep anxieties about her body. And you're wondering how you can help.

Most of us, at some point, fall into unhealthy habits around food or exercise. So it's helpful to know that doctors distinguish between disordered eating and eating disorders.[16] Disordered eating can include eating due to boredom or stress, labeling foods as good and bad, or skipping meals. All these habits may be unhelpful, but they haven't progressed to a truly dangerous spot.

Eating disorders, on the other hand, are a medical

diagnosis requiring treatment. They often involve similar behaviors, but now those behaviors and habits are more frequent and more obsessive, and pose a significant threat to the body's health.

Our culture is filled with examples encouraging disordered eating habits—and we've talked about many of those habits elsewhere in this book. But sometimes disordered eating habits can grow into a full eating disorder. So, what do we do if we fear that might be the case for us or someone we love?

This is not meant to be an exhaustive response, or take the place of advice from a medical or eating-disorder specialist. I will refer you elsewhere for the expert opinions you need. But I am someone who has walked closely with a dear friend struggling in these areas for years. This section is intended to point you in the right direction on the pathway to freedom, and to remind you that you're not alone—God is here to help you, every step along the way.

DIAGNOSTIC QUESTIONS

First off, here are some questions to ask yourself, to help you determine if your food or exercise has become a serious problem.

- Can I enjoy the food placed before me without worrying about how to burn off the calories?
- Do I miss out on social events, church fellowships and dinners with friends because I'm concerned about the food they serve (how it is prepared, if it is healthy enough)?
- Do I feel like I have to burn a certain number of calories each day?

- Am I consumed with thoughts about my body image?
- Am I always trying to lose weight, hopping from diet to diet?
- Is my day ruined if I miss my workout?
- Do I push my body with physical exercise to the point of utter exhaustion or physical injury?
- Can I take a day to rest from my exercise routine without anxiety?
- Is my day ruined if I eat something not on my "safe" food list? Do I feel guilty about what I eat?
- Do I restrict certain types of food and binge on others?
- Do I feel out of control around certain types of food?
- Do I eat in secret or hide the evidence of what I've been eating? Do I feel shame and remorse afterward?
- Do I unnecessarily restrict entire food groups without the recommendation of a medical provider?

Remember, most of us experience symptoms of disordered eating at one point or another. You don't need to freak out if you answered "yes" to any of those questions! At the same time, if you did answer "yes," it should be a red flag that something is off with how you're viewing food, exercise, and your body.

You might be surprised by how prevalent eating disorders are in the Western world. Although they're more common among females, a growing number of males also have an eating disorder. Approximately 20 million girls and women and 10 million boys and men in America have an eating disorder.[17]

You likely know some of the names of eating disorders already. But there are other, less well-known eating disorders too—so just because you don't fit the stereotype of an anorexia or bulimia sufferer, don't dismiss the possibility that you or your loved one may need medical help. The National Eating Disorders Association website is a great place to go to help you find out more.[18]

If you think it's possible that you or someone you love may be one of the millions of eating-disorder sufferers, you should know that eating disorders are treatable. You don't need to be ashamed or afraid. If you have recognized that eating may be a much bigger issue for you than you previously realized, that's a great first step. You're already on the path to freedom.

So, what do you do next?

THE PATHWAY TO FREEDOM

1. Make an appointment with your doctor

Eating disorders affect both your brain and your body. These are mental disorders manifested in the physical body through excessive food restriction, binging, compulsive exercise, and a distorted view of the body. Sometimes it takes a medical doctor to point out the stunted growth of a teenage girl who isn't consuming enough calories, or the high cholesterol and weight gain compounded by excessive eating, or the physical injury derived from pushing a body beyond its limits in exercise.

I remember my friend Jane, who took her teenage daughter, Ellie, for her yearly physical. Because my friend saw her daughter every day, she didn't notice the slow decline in her weight. It seemed like Ellie was just on a health kick—choosing not to eat anything with sugar or carbs, making sure she exercised regularly. But sometimes the fads of today can hide the symptoms of an eating disorder. Ellie's changing body was being deprived of important nutrients she needed to grow. When the doctor mentioned the word anorexia, Jane was stunned—and embarrassed that she hadn't detected it herself. The doctor recommended a counselor for Ellie who was trained to help with eating disorders. And so they began the long path forward to recovery.

You might not be sure whether or not you have an eating disorder. Don't be afraid to speak to a doctor and ask for his or her expert advice. It's their job to help you!

2. Find a counselor with specialized training

It may be hard to know where to look when you're in the midst of suffering and looking for fast help. Not to mention trying to figure out which counselors are covered by your insurance. Not all counselors are educated in how to help those with eating disorders. In the US, you can use the website *map.nationaleatingdisorders.org* to find links to counselors specially trained in eating-disorder recovery.

3. Share the struggle with a trusted friend, pastor, or biblical counselor

We aren't meant to walk through our trials alone. The beauty of the church is that we are called to "bear one another's burdens" (Galatians 6:2). We need the listening ear, the prayers, and the unconditional love of others in the body of Christ to hold up our weary arms when we feel like quitting.

So, can you think of a mature Christian friend whom you trust to talk to about your struggles? This may be a small-group leader, a pastor, a family member, or friend. Bear in mind that most of these people won't be trained in how to talk about eating disorders—they likely won't be able to give you medical advice and they may not fully understand what you're experiencing. But it's also true that these struggles are not merely mental or physical but also spiritual. It can be invaluable to have a mature Christian friend to pray with you, help you evaluate the counsel you're receiving, provide accountability, and be a steady source of encouragement, pointing you back to the truths of Scripture.

It may also help to find a Christian counselor who can help you think things through from a biblical standpoint. The Christian Counseling and Education Foundation and the Association of Biblical Counselors both have directories of available counselors.[19]

4. Cry out to the Lord for help, trusting he will grant mercy to help in time of need (Hebrews 4:16)

The Lord longs for you to pour out your heart to him. He is a compassionate and merciful Lord, quick to forgive and eager to give us strength in our weakness. Remember that he desires you to live in freedom and provides the Holy Spirit to help you!

Recovering from an eating disorder is not an overnight fix. For many people, it requires years of work, professional help and persevering through failures and setbacks. Yet recovery is possible! I would recommend the book *Table for Two*, in which author Krista Dunham candidly shares about her 10-year recovery process from an eating disorder. She praises God that she can now sit at the dinner table with her husband and children and genuinely enjoy the food set before her, free from the worries and fears that used to plague her.[20]

God does not leave us to battle this alone. Instead he provides the Holy Spirit to help us, giving us self-control in our moments of weakness and the peace and joy that come from following the Lord wholeheartedly. Jesus came to set us free from the power of sin and death. While you're in the midst of your disorder you might feel enslaved, you can trust that God can set you free. He will make a way even when it seems like there is no way.

> *"Behold, I am doing a new thing; now it springs*
> *forth, do you not perceive it? I will make a way in*
> *the wilderness and rivers in the desert."*
>
> *(Isaiah 43:19)*

Pour out your heart to the Lord, tell him your fears, your worries, and your hopes, and bank on the promise that he will be your refuge and strength, an ever-present help in trouble (Psalm 46:1).

A WORD TO MOMS

I have two daughters, one who just exited the teenage years and one who is in the midst of them. I've watched up close how our girls are surrounded by pressure. Pressure to look a certain way, to measure up to the girl posting the filtered selfie on social media, to eat certain foods, to wear fashionable clothes, and to be in the "right" group of friends. Honestly I really can't imagine a more difficult time to be a teenage girl. Thankfully I didn't grow up in the world of social media (and it was *still* hard to not compare myself with others!). Our girls today face an extra pressure, and we as moms can add to the pressure—or take the pressure off—without knowing it.

One day after church a small group of women gathered together in our church parking lot, chatting. It was shortly after Covid and the notorious topic of quarantine weight gain had become the central discussion. As women shared about their newest baking feats, they inevitably ended up sharing about their weight gain as well. My teenage daughter walked up to the circle, eager to join in the conversation, but she remained silent. Right then and there I knew I needed to change the direction of the conversation, but it was already too late. Later that day my daughter approached me: "Mom, why is it that women are always talking about how much they weigh? Or the foods they made that are either 'so bad' or super healthy?"

My heart sank, knowing that this conversation had not helped my daughter to accept her changing body with a glad heart, but instead had put questions and doubts in her mind: what really is "overweight"? What foods are ok to eat without feeling guilty?

My point is, our daughters are watching us. They're listening to our conversations in the church parking lot. They notice when we complain about our pants being too tight or the latest wrinkle on our faces. And no matter how hard I've tried to avoid these kinds of comments, I know that I've made unhelpful remarks. Thankfully, God gives grace for our mistakes: he can redeem our mom failures! But I do want to encourage you to make your home one that doesn't focus on commenting on outward appearances—either yours or others'.

Instead of commenting on how Aunt Suzanne looks like she lost weight, consider complimenting a character trait you see in her. Yes, tell your daughters they are beautiful, but praise even louder the acts of courage and compassion you see in their lives. Notice when they sacrifice their own good for the sake of another. Tell them how you see God working in them, making them more beautiful inwardly as they grow more like Jesus.

Let's teach our daughters not just by our words, but even more by our example.

Acknowledgments

I'm so grateful for the opportunity to write *Beautiful Freedom*. The words in this book have been swirling around in my mind and heart for years. What a privilege it was to put pen to paper, trusting that the Lord has a purpose for this book beyond what I can imagine.

To the women who shared their stories with me—thank you for your transparency and your willingness to share some of your hardest seasons for the sake of helping others. May the words of 2 Corinthians 1:4 prove true—that you may be able to comfort others in affliction with the comfort that you have received from God.

To Katy Morgan—thank you for your patience, diligence, and careful editing, which make this book so much better. I enjoyed all our zoom meetings and getting a peek into British life (and phrases!).

To the entire team at The Good Book Company—thank you for your excitement and belief in this project and all your efforts to get the word out.

To Don Gates—thank you for championing this book and helping me navigate the publishing world.

To Faith Walker, Kimberly Bello, and Jen Oshman— thank you for reading early versions of the manuscript and tricky chapters, sharpening me with fresh insights and words of encouragement when I needed them most.

To my teaching comrade, Erica Oshlick—thank you for your support and encouragement both in the classroom and with my writing. Tuesdays and Thursdays are brighter because of you.

To the saints at Three Rivers Grace Church—thank you for your constant prayers throughout the writing process, for asking me, "How's the book going?" at church or small group, and for rejoicing with me when the final edits were turned in.

To my parents, Ralph and Nancy Kyro, and my in-laws, Ron and Barbara Reaoch—thank you for your unfailing support, encouragement, and prayers, which fueled this project. What a gift to know you are always in my corner!

To my children—Milaina, Noah, Annalyse and Micah—you are four of my greatest treasures. I'm so grateful to be your mom. Thank you for your enthusiasm over my writing, for sharing your insights on these topics, and for giving me grace when my writing time took longer than expected.

To my husband, Ben—you are the reason this book exists. Thank you for sacrificially serving our family to help me find time to write. Thank you for always being my first reader and editor, sharpening me theologically, and putting down your book to listen to my rambling thoughts and words. You are the best husband I could ask for, and I love you more than words can say.

And to my Lord and Savior, Jesus—writing a book reminds me of my dependence on you for every word and breath. You've saved me, upheld me, comforted me, and guided me. May the words of this book bring you honor and praise as women embrace the freedom that you've purchased for us.

Notes

1   www.dictionary.com/browse/beauty (accessed on Sept. 23, 2022).

2   Elyse Fitzpatrick, *Idols of the Heart* (P&R Publishing, 2001), p 23.

3   Tim Keller, *Counterfeit Gods* (Penguin, 2009), p xvii.

4   See Elyse Fitzpatrick, *Idols of the Heart*, p 20-23.

5   Tim Keller, *Counterfeit Gods*, p 172.

6   Scott Hubbard's article "Let There Be Rest: Recovering Healthy Weekly Rhythms" (Desiring God, Aug. 29, 2021) was very helpful to me in thinking all of this through. See www.desiringgod.org/articles/let-there-be-rest (accessed on Aug. 21, 2023).

7   Much of what follows has been adapted from a blog I wrote for Desiring God: "Exercise for More of God" (May 16, 2019): www.desiringgod.org/articles/exercise-for-more-of-god (accessed on Aug. 7, 2023).

8   "Is Body Image My Idol?" Interview with John Piper (Desiring God, May 17, 2017): www.desiringgod.org/interviews/is-body-image-my-idol (accessed on Aug. 7, 2023).

9   *A Narrative of Some of the Lord's Dealings with George Müller, Written By Himself* (Dust and Ashes, 2003), 1:271.

10 Scientific research has proven exercise to be a means of fighting depression—see Shona Murray's book *Refresh* (Crossway, 2017), p 72.

11 See Asheritah Ciuciu, *Full* (Moody, 2017), p 155.

12 Elyse Fitzpatrick, *Love to Eat, Hate to Eat* (Harvest House, 1999), p 125.

13 John Piper, *A Hunger for God* (Crossway, 1997), p 15.

14 "How Can I Conquer Gluttony?" Interview with John Piper (Desiring God, Jan. 2, 2008): www.desiringgod.org/inter-views/how-can-i-conquer-gluttony (accessed on Apr. 13, 2023).

15 Interview with Justine Bateman on *Today* (April 3, 2023): www.today.com/health/aging/justine-bateman-embracing-ag-ing-really-fear-rcna77872 (accessed on May 22, 2023).

16 You can find a definition by Kristen Fuller, MD, in an article from June 28, 2022 on the website Very Well Mind: www.verywellmind.com/difference-between-disordered-eat-ing-and-eating-disorders-5184548 (accessed on Jul. 5, 2023).

17 my.clevelandclinic.org/health/diseases/4152-eating-disorders (accessed on Jul. 5, 2023).

18 www.nationaleatingdisorders.org/what-are-eating-disorders (accessed on Jul. 25, 2023).

19 See www.ccef.org/find-a-counselor-near-you and www.chris-tiancounseling.com.

20 David and Krista Dunham, *Table for Two* (New Growth Press, 2021), p 93.

the good book

C O M P A N Y

BIBLICAL | RELEVANT | ACCESSIBLE

At The Good Book Company, we are dedicated to helping Christians and local churches grow. We believe that God's growth process always starts with hearing clearly what he has said to us through his timeless word—the Bible.

Ever since we opened our doors in 1991, we have been striving to produce Bible-based resources that bring glory to God. We have grown to become an international provider of user-friendly resources to the Christian community, with believers of all backgrounds and denominations using our books, Bible studies, devotionals, evangelistic resources, and DVD-based courses.

We want to equip ordinary Christians to live for Christ day by day, and churches to grow in their knowledge of God, their love for one another, and the effectiveness of their outreach.

Call us for a discussion of your needs or visit one of our local websites for more information on the resources and services we provide.

Your friends at The Good Book Company

thegoodbook.com | thegoodbook.co.uk
thegoodbook.com.au | thegoodbook.co.nz
thegoodbook.co.in